Your
Heart's
Desire

ALSO BY SONIA CHOQUETTE

All of the above are available at your
local bookstore, or may be ordered by visiting:

Hay House UK: www.hayhouse.co.uk
Hay House USA: www.hayhouse.com®
Hay House Australia: www.hayhouse.com.au
Hay House South Africa: www.hayhouse.co.za
Hay House India: www.hayhouse.co.in

Your Heart's Desire

Instructions for Creating the
Life You Really Want

SONIA CHOQUETTE

Meditations by
PATRICK TULLY
Foreword by
JULIA CAMERON

HAY HOUSE
Australia • Canada • Hong Kong • India
South Africa • United Kingdom • United States

Originally published and distributed in the United States of America by:
Three Rivers Press, New York, New York. A Member of the Crown Publishing Group.

First published and distributed in the United Kingdom by:
Hay House UK Ltd, 292B Kensal Rd, London W10 5BE. Tel.: (44) 20 8962 1230;
Fax: (44) 20 8962 1239. www.hayhouse.co.uk

Published and distributed in Australia by:
Hay House Australia Ltd, 18/36 Ralph St, Alexandria NSW 2015. Tel.: (61) 2 9669 4299;
Fax: (61) 2 9669 4144. www.hayhouse.com.au

Published and distributed in the Republic of South Africa by:
Hay House SA (Pty), Ltd, PO Box 990, Witkoppen 2068. Tel./Fax: (27) 11 467 8904.
www.hayhouse.co.za

Published and distributed in India by:
Hay House Publishers India, Muskaan Complex, Plot No.3, B-2, Vasant Kunj, New Delhi
– 110 070. Tel.: (91) 11 4176 1620; Fax: (91) 11 4176 1630. www.hayhouse.co.in

Distributed in Canada by:
Raincoast, 9050 Shaughnessy St, Vancouver, BC V6P 6E5. Tel.: (1) 604 323 7100;
Fax: (1) 604 323 2600

A catalogue record for this book is available from the British Library.

ISBN 978-1-84850-272-7

Printed and bound in Great Britain by TJ International, Padstow, Cornwall.

This book is dedicated to my mom and dad, who taught me not only to wish on a star, but also how to reach for one; and to Kathy Churay, who helped me transform these Principles from wishes and dreams into my own realized Heart's Desire. May I one day be able to repay you all for your generosity and support.

ACKNOWLEDGMENTS

I would like to thank my husband and partner, Patrick Tully, for so lovingly creating with me all that our hearts have desired, beginning with his work in designing the first Heart's Desire workshops in 1980. It was his focus and belief in these principles that allowed this work to evolve into a book.

To my children, who demonstrate daily the belief in dreams, magic, and the magnificent healing power of love.

To my parents, who live these principles without hesitation and opened up the world of possibility to me from the very beginning of my journey.

To my dear friend and mentor, Julia Cameron, for helping me find my voice. Without her, neither of my books would exist.

To the rest of my spiritual family—my sister, Cuky Harvey, LuAnn Glatzmaier, Joan Smith, Shenoa Grace, Wendy Taylor, and Bill Mondi—for sharing my visions, believing in these principles, and lighting my way when I became lost in doubt.

To Susan Schulman, my terrific agent, who spirited this work into the right hands.

To Gail Seminara-Mandel and Howard Mandel at Transitions Bookplace, for their unflagging confidence in my work and for giving it a royal introduction to readers in Chicago.

To those at Crown and Clarkson Potter who have believed in me, and have taken these principles and carefully and lovingly crafted them into this solid work. To Chip Gibson, my publisher at Three Rivers Press, for believing in this project and giving it the power for realization. To Carol Southern, my brilliant and grounded editor. To Camille Smith for attending to the details, and Jane Treuhaft for surrounding this work with beauty. To Amy Zelvin, my publicist, for paving its way into the world, and to Joy Sikorski for overseeing it to the end.

And to Amber Arnett, my assistant, for suffering through the trials, celebrating the victories, and balancing me in the process. You are a saint.

Together you magnificently embody the universal principles at their best.

My final thanks pours out to all my clients, whose adventures have taught me so much, and who serve as the best of teachers to me.

To Dr. Trenton Tully, Charlie Goodman, and all my spiritual helpers, I thank you from the bottom of my heart.

CONTENTS

FOREWORD

Dear Readers,

Ours is an age when many of us feel out of control, victimized by the velocity and direction of modern life. Too much seems to be happening to us that is not of our own making. We are swept along, buffeted and bruised by the velocity of world events. Many of us long for a life that is more handmade, perhaps simpler but certainly more personal, more satisfying than the life we seem to be leading by default.

"I want more of what I want in my life—and less of everything else," we say, but we do not know how to effect this change. This is where the work of Sonia Choquette comes in.

All too often we are told that we should lead lives that are more spiritual and yet are also more fulfilled in worldly terms. Frankly, we would love to—if someone would just tell us how. What we want and need is nuts-and-bolts information on how to build such a life. We don't just need the vision of the life we could and should have. We want the actual feast, not the images and picture and descriptions of it. What we want—and what we deserve—is the actual recipe.

Sonia Choquette is not only a master spiritual teacher, she is a teacher who shares her recipe for living in a series of clear, simple, doable steps. Not for her the grand, highbrow, and elusive evocation of how wonderful it could be if we would just somehow get spiritual. Instead, Choqette brings spirituality into practice. This means she gets practical. She gets nuts-and-bolts. She gets nitty-gritty. She doesn't just tell us to do something. She tells us exactly *how* to do it.

The book market is flooded with spiritual self-help books that are not particularly helpful. They promise to tell us how to function in seven simple laws or twenty-one wizardly ways, but when we look at the laws or ways closely, they are difficult to integrate into life as we know it. "Meditate an hour a day." Sure, if you find me that hour.

Choquette gives spiritual direction in bite-size chunks. Married, the mother of two, a full-time writer, spiritual teacher, and practicing intuitive, she has had to learn the art and the skills of time management for modern life. Her books teach what she herself has had to learn: how to "do" a fulfilling life somewhere in the middle of the life you've actually got.

For the past decade, Choquette has been a close friend of mine. Over time I have realized her considerable education, erudition, and sophistication (her tone is a well-polished jewel of cosmopolitan taste). I have come to appreciate that her grounded, humorous, populist approach to spirituality is a carefully chosen path. She teaches through story and principle rather than steeping her work in the intellectualism and borrowed respectability that so many people use to mask and promote their message.

Reading Sonia Choquette will not make you feel smart. Reading Sonia Choquette will make you *be* smart. When a friend or student hits troubled water and needs to revamp a badly damaged sense of life safety, I do not send him to the best-selling spiritual gurus of our time, fine writers and teachers though they are. Over and over, for soul hunger, it is to Choquette's work that I send people who genuinely want their own lives to alter and expand. I do this because Choquette is an empowering teacher. She teaches people to trust themselves, not her. She is, to my eye, radically humble: "Be your own guru," she advises, and then adds, "Here's how."

With every hope that Sonia's work is as valuable in your life as it has been in mine.

Julia Cameron

INTRODUCTION

As I reflect on how this book came to be, a profound sense of gratitude sweeps over me for all my teachers, both on the physical plans and in spirit. This book truly exists as my own manifested miracle, my Heart's Desire fulfilled.

Let me tell you how it came to be written.

Many years ago, when I first began doing intuitive readings, I found that the most difficult part of my task was having to tell some of my clients that the things they wanted weren't going to happen for them. Every time this occurred, I felt as though I were crushing their hopes, and I hated doing it. After a few painful years of "shoot the messenger" experiences, I decided that there must be a better way to help people. I felt I was failing to do my job correctly if I was merely forecasting failure, not counseling toward success. If I couldn't do that, I wasn't helping anyone at all. In fact, I might even be setting clients back by my discouraging words.

That thought really bothered me. Being intuitive was fulfilling, but my work was incomplete. I could not continue to be merely an intuitive voyeur. When I perceived my clients' disappointments, I wanted to be able to offer genuine guidance in the form of solutions. I just had to learn what those solutions were. And as soon as I focused on my goal, the entire universe of spiritual learning opened up to me.

My learning process has been aided by Divine spirit from the very beginning of my life. My first teacher was my own mother. Having surmounted incredible obstacles as a child in war-torn Europe during World War II, she served as an example of possibility and persistence for me. Through her I learned the power of intention and imagination and was taught to believe the world was willing to embrace and support all that I could imagine, if I was willing to do my part.

With her blessing and camaraderie, my pursuit of knowledge led me further into the stuff of religion, metaphysics, and spiritual development. As I studied, I began to understand that awareness was the hidden key to success. Entering into this domain, I felt like a kid wandering into a candy store. I was passionate about my studies. In my enthusiasm for answers, I studied astrology, numerology, tarot, cabala, auras, meditation, yoga, the chakra system, and anything else that seemed relevant to teach me how spirit creates in the earthly domain. I left no stone unturned. Slowly, as if piecing together a huge puzzle, I began to discover how anyone can create what they want.

During this time I was also introduce to my two spiritual mentors, Charlie Goodman and Dr. Trenton Tully. Under their guidance I was taught the truth that as spiritual beings "in the image and likeness of God," we are indeed the creative architects of our life experience. More important, I learned that the process that directs a creative impulse into a manifested outcome is consistent, consecutive, and impartial. With my teachers' help, I learned these principles in theory. Since then I have spent my life putting these principles into practice. In doing so, I have experienced miracle after miracle. I have been amazed and delighted, and those around me have been astounded at my consistent "good luck."

Finally, fourteen years ago, I felt compelled to share what I had learned with my clients. At first I began introducing the Principles of Creativity to them one on one in their readings. I would help them identify which Principles they needed to engage in order to stay on their path and realize their dreams. Soon, however, I realized that it would be far better to teach these Principles to people by presenting them in their entirety.

My husband, Patrick, and I designed a workshop called "The Nature of Reality: How to Create What You Want." Initially this workshop was complex and overwhelming, but over time, with practice and the help of our students, we simplified it until we had refined and distilled the workshop into simple, clear directives, taking the essence of broad universal teachings and making them concise, practical, and easy to follow. This new format provided any student who wanted to create a dream a Divine escort to fulfillment.

And so this book came to be. It is a synthesis of all that I have studied for over twenty-five years. I have modeled it after the tree of life in the cabala, an ancient metaphysical system for the transformation process of creativity.

This book embodies my interpretations of complex spiritual laws and their application. I have chosen to write it in a simple workbook format that illustrates each Principle with stories. As you will see in the text, my greatest spiritual influences are Jesus of Nazareth and Gautama Buddha, who both taught in parables. In my text I use modern-day parables drawn from my own students, clients, and personal experiences.

I believe there are principles still waiting to be learned, and I await them with an open and eager heart. What I have learned so far has been better than a magic lantern and has lighted my way for over twenty years. My learning has blessed my life, and though far from complete, it is my Heart's Desire to share it with others.

The following Principles of Creativity have provided me with innumerable miracles, joyous surprises, and a profound sense of abundance, security, and peace. Through working with them, I've learned that if I'm willing to do my part, then God will meet me halfway. For over twenty years I have experienced the universal love and goodness these Principles bring, surrounding me with all that my heart has ever truly desired. In the same spirit of love and generosity in which I was given this knowledge, I want to share these Principles with you. In their simplicity, they work miracles.

The key to their success is to follow the Principles one by one, in order. The successful completion of each Principle will naturally lead you to the next. If you stumble along the way, simply go back to the beginning and review the Principles to make sure you have thoroughly absorbed each one. Keep a journal with all the exercises in the book that you can refer to later.

If you are the type of person who starts but doesn't finish things, or if you get easily distracted or discouraged, it will help you to stay on course if you find a trusted friend or two who will work on these Principles along with you.

Please note that you do *not* have to rush through them. It's better to take your time, applying each Principle correctly, than to push through anxiously, working in the wrong direction.

Try the Principles yourself and see what happens. I believe with all my heart that they will work for you as well. These Principles have led me to experience a joyous and miraculous life. In wishing the same for you, I have created this manual. I hope it will lead you to your dreams.

Warming Up

Before you begin to work on your dreams and desires, you need to follow three simple rules.

RULE #1: TRAVEL LIGHTLY

If you want to move toward your dream, don't be attached to your fears. As you enter into this creative journey to the heart, leave behind all your presumptions about the way life works. Don't burden yourself with useless notions, secondhand opinions, or "reality" as other people have explained to you. You can create whatever you desire as long as you apply the Universal Principles of Creativity. There is no favoritism involved and no luck. There is, however, synchronicity and grace. If you follow the natural Principles of Creativity, you will receive these gifts along the way.

Enter into your creative mission knowing you are a spiritual being here on earth to express your creative divinity and remember who you are.

RULE #2: TAKE RESPONSIBILITY FOR YOUR DREAM

In order to create your dream, you must first recognize that you are a Divine creator and as such have *already* created many miracles in your life; even the circumstances you don't like are reflections of your creativity. This means that you can't blame others, deny responsibility, point fingers, feel sorry for yourself, or allow yourself to be angry over the way your life is now.

In other words, take responsibility for yourself and admire the life you've already manifested... even if it's in a terrible mess. Even a mess takes creativity to happen. Look at every aspect of your life dispassionately; good, bad, or indifferent, it has your indelible mark of personal and unique creativity. If your life conditions aren't satisfying, then decide to *create* something else. After all, no matter what your life situation, you can turn it into something better if you aren't stuck on how bad it is today.

My mother used to say to us, "Bless your mess." In other words, there's no point in wasting your emotions on being upset. More important, don't waste your time on raging or blaming others for where you are. If you do, you surrender to them all your creative power, and I can assure you, they will *not* use it to make you any happier.

You might be tempted to ask, "You mean I'm responsible for my unfair boss, my abusive spouse, my poor health, my awful job?"

Not at all. But your creativity put you in that situation, and your creativity can get you out of it. No matter where you are in life today, nothing can really stop you from realizing your dream tomorrow. Even a horrible scenario holds the potential for you to tap the most profound genius in yourself.

Let's face it, we all tend to cruise creatively when things are going well. It's when we are under fire that the wheels in the creative mind start turning.

My mother told me a story once that illustrated this point. A Romanian by birth, she was imprisoned in a concentration camp as a child during World War II. Through her soulful good fortune and intuitive ingenuity, she managed to survive.

After the American troops arrived, my mother was liberated from the camp and set free in the small Bavarian town nearby. To restore order, the army put a very strict martial law into effect. The countryside had been decimated by the war, and everyone was scrambling for food, clothing, and supplies. According to my mother, this put everyone "at their very *best* creative incentive."

A friend of hers, a Gypsy names Larosh, managed to steal an army blanket, which was strictly against army rules. The weather was freezing cold, and supplies fell far short of even the soldier's needs. Unfortunately Larosh was spotted with the blanket and arrested. Such an infraction merited three months in the military prison—and he had been caught red-handed.

My mother and several others got together to try to think of a way to get Larosh out of jail, racking their brains for possible excuses for his theft. Finally my mother came up with an idea. She suggested that at his court hearing he should say he was color-blind and could not tell that the blanket he had stolen was an army blanket.

What a creative explanation! The court must have thought so, too, because they accepted his story. Larosh was set free.

My mother said this kind of brainstorming brought out the best creativity in everyone. People had no time to be angry or feel sorry for themselves. If they wanted to survive, they had to use their creative energy to think of ways to do so. Even though the problems seemed too much to bear for any one person, they banded together and became more clever by the day. Little things, like finding a potato or an egg, became major victories.

Surrendering your power over to blame, resentment, or anger or feeling like a victim is the worst thing you can do. Wherever you are, use your situation as a launching pad to fly toward your dream.

RULE #3: DON'T BE A CONTROL FREAK!

Being a control freak means that you want guarantees of success before you take a risk. It means you want to avoid all potential injury or disappointment before you try. It means needing to know you'll succeed before you even begin. But above all it means *failure*, because the kind of assurance the control freak wants is an earned gift, the product of courage and risk, which cannot be attained in advance.

Wanting the promise of a certain outcome means that you limit what you give and in turn diminish what you get. Finally, avoiding disappointment means avoiding life itself, because disappointment is a necessary teacher to let us know when we fall off our path and need to take a new direction.

If you are a control freak, you cannot create freely, because creating freely comes from your real essence, your true self—your soul. Creating from a controlling perspective means trying to create out of your ego, and you cannot create real Heart's Desires out of ego. Real Heart's Desires are the expressions of the soul.

These are the three simple rules to keep in mind as you take the steps to create your dream. My favorite line from the I-Ching says it all: "If the beginning is right, the ending is right." So in order to ensure a wonderful beginning: (1) travel lightly; (2) take responsibility for your dream; and (3) don't be a control freak.

You Are a Divine Creator Now

Before you begin to work on your Heart's Desire, it is very important to recognize the creative successes you've already had. List all of your greatest achievements, from birth until the present, as a way of acknowledging your creative power in action.

PRINCIPLE NUMBER ONE

Bring Your Dream into Focus

The First Principle of Creativity simply states that your *thought* creates. Therefore if you want to create an experience, you must begin by having a clear, focused thought of that experience. The First Principle also states that *whatever* you clearly focus on, you do create, whether or not you want to.

Desire directs focus. If your desires are vague, your focus will be blurred. If your desires are heartfelt, however, your focus will be sharp and clear. That's why vague desires will never materialize, but clearly focused Heart's Desires will. Clear focus is the mind's magic wand. It points your creativity in a particular direction and channels your experience behind it. Wherever you clearly focus, you create.

I first learned this lesson as a teenager from my mom. I remember going to her one day, heartbroken because the tenth-grade prom was fast approaching and I didn't have a date. To add to my frustration, platform shoes were essential during my high school years, and the average height of my male classmates at the primarily Hispanic school I attended was all of five and a half feet! At five feet eight inches and wearing platforms, I was a towering six-foot wallflower no one would dance with. I felt like Cinderella, overlooked and rejected while everyone else was getting ready for the ball.

My mom listened sympathetically to my plight but didn't give me the response I expected.

"I'm not surprised no one has asked you to the prom," she said.

"After all, you're creating your problem by *focusing* on how short the boys are and how awkward you feel. Your focus drives them away. Why not focus on meeting someone tall enough so you can wear your shoes and go to the prom? Sharpen your focus on creating a tall prince to take you to the ball!"

"How?" I cried. "I only have three weeks before the prom. I don't have time to focus on creating anything!"

"Oh yes, you do," she said. "Magic can happen in a moment."

Not wanting to be left behind, I decided to give it a try.

My focus began with envisioning a cute guy picking me up and taking me to the prom. Like a movie running through my mind, I created someone very tall so I could wear my platform shoes and not tower over him. (The platforms may sound unimportant now, but in fact they were crucial. At sixteen my outfit was everything, and the platform shoes were the most important part. If you didn't have *the shoes*, you simply weren't cool.)

Focusing on my dream date consumed my attention for the next two weeks. At times I wrote a list of my prince's qualities— tall, cute, good dancer. At other times I sketched him in my notebook—long hair, thin, with David Bowie looks. I even confided to a girlfriend what I was up to and recruited her to the cause. We'd each take turns describing to the other our vision of "my guy" in lengthy, delicious detail, almost squirming with delight as our focus became more and more developed.

I saw him in my mind's eye the moment I woke up every morning. I drifted off to sleep every night as I imagined him picking me up in a stretch limousine. Why not? It was my movie. I looked for him around every corner. I expected him at any moment. I put myself into quite a state waiting for him to show up.

I did this for two whole weeks, confident in the outcome. But in spite of all my efforts, "he" didn't show up as I expected. As I entered the final week before the prom, my spirits began to drop. My confidence crumbled. My focus faded into disillusionment.

Three days before the prom and still no date, I couldn't stand it anymore.

"Forget it!" I announced to myself that morning as my imagination geared up for its now familiar ritual. "I don't even want to go to the stupid prom."

The looming disappointment was too much to bear. I decided I'd buy a new pair of shoes to console myself and go to the movies instead.

After work the next afternoon I went to a new shoe store nearby to check out the shoes. There, sitting on display, was the most beautiful pair of platforms I'd ever seen. They were white, glittery rhinestone shoes with blue acrylic six-inch soles.

Outstanding! I had to have them.

As I held them, my heart sank as I thought about how perfect they would have been for the prom I wouldn't be attending. I took the shoes to the counter and waited for a salesman. After a couple of minutes the cutest guy I'd ever seen emerged from behind the curtain. Long blond hair, six feet five, skinny, and wearing a *very* cool pair of plaid platforms himself—he looked like David Bowie. The sight of him took my breath away.

"Can I help you?" he asked, whisking the sample shoes out of my hands. "Isn't this the best shoe in the store? It just arrived today. Want to try it?"

A little embarrassed at my reaction to him, I said, "Sure, why not?" When he returned with the pair of shoes for me to try on, I had composed myself. I slipped the shoe on. It fit like a glove.

"You gotta buy this shoe," he said. "It's just too cool to pass up. Walk around. Let me admire you."

I loved both the shoes and the salesman, but... "I can't buy these," I said, coming back to reality. "They're very expensive and

I have no place to wear them."

"If you buy these shoes," he said, "I'll take you anywhere you want to go." I noticed as he spoke that I was looking *up* to him!

"I don't believe you," I said. "You're just trying to get a sale!"

"No, really. Where do you want to go?"

"The ball," I responded jokingly.

"Okay, to the ball." He laughed. "When?"

I blushed. "Well..." I summoned my courage. "There *is* my school prom on Saturday night, but I'm sure you have plans." How could someone this cute not have plans?

"No, I don't have plans. I'd be honored. Just tell me where to be."

Within minutes I had a date to the prom and new glass (rhinestone) slippers to wear. On Saturday night my prince arrived in his father's yellow Cadillac. It wasn't a limo, but it was close enough for me. The best part was that as I arrived to greet him at the door, I noticed that in addition to his beautiful tuxedo, he wore a marvelous pair of glittery red rhinestone platforms to match my own. Together we shimmered off to the ball in style and had a fantastic time—so much so that we dated all through my high school years.

If I had any doubts before about the power of focus, they were forever banished.

Try it yourself and see!

HOW DO YOU KNOW WHAT TO FOCUS ON?

It is my experience as a teacher of the Principles of Creativity that often people do *not* really know what their heart desires. In fact, they have no idea at all.

When you think of the word "desire" you think of passion, yearning, intense longing. When you have a true desire, you have a burning urge for some particular experience or outcome. This burning, intense, passionate longing is the creative spark that sets miracle making into motion. Without it, nothing gets going. If you do not have this spark of authentic intensity, your creative miracle-making process will lie dormant.

Blurry, disjointed ideas lack the necessary spark to set your energy into motion. True Heart's Desires are felt in the present moment and reflect your most immediate needs and concerns. If you are blocked or confused about your true Heart's Desires, start by looking at your immediate life and ask yourself what you need. Honestly assess what's missing. Is there anything specific you are waiting for? Is there anything you aren't noticing because it is *so* obvious that you overlook it?

Don't laugh. Sometimes we overlook our deepest desires because they're hiding in plain sight.

A client of mine named Lorraine came up to me on a break from the Heart's Desire workshop.

"I think I'd better leave," she said. "Everyone here is so clear about what they want to create, yet I don't have *any* ideas at all."

"Lorraine, before you go, let me ask you. Why did you come? What brought you here in the first place?"

"Frustration," Lorraine answered. "I thought maybe I'd get some inspiration, because I just feel rushed and empty all the time. It's depressing!"

"Well, perhaps you can uncover some clue to your Heart's Desire by noticing what is depressing you," I suggested. "What is missing in your life?" What do you *not* experience now?"

"One thing missing is fun!" she groaned. "I don't get any pleasure from my life at all."

"What does fun mean to you? What would you enjoy experiencing, let's say, tomorrow?"

"I can't even answer that because no matter what I can think of, I couldn't do it anyway!"

"Why not? What's stopping you?"

"Responsibility! I have responsibilities. I have three boys who have soccer baseball, homework... I have laundry, dinner, dishes, a part-time job, and my husband won't help. So I *cannot* have fun. It's not possible. I don't have time."

"That's your clue, Lorraine," I said. "Sounds to me like your Heart's Desire would be to get some help in managing your family's agenda so you can have time for yourself. What if that were your goal?"

"That *would* be a miracle!" She smiled, exasperated. "I never thought of that. It seems like such a mundane goal. I though Heart's Desires were more glamorous. This seems too practical."

"Well, that's what the Principles are all about—creating the miracle you *need.*"

Lorraine decided to focus on the miracle of getting someone to clean the house and run errands, because that was what she really needed. She just didn't see it.

Was it a true goal?

Absolutely.

WHAT IF YOU ARE CONFUSED ABOUT WHAT YOU DESIRE?

Often my clients have felt unclear about whether the things they want are their true Heart's Desires. For example, after taking the Heart's Desires workshop, Carol came to me for a private consultation because she felt quite confused.

"I thought my goal was to marry my boyfriend, James," she said, "but three months ago I broke off our engagement because I wasn't feeling comfortable with the idea of marrying him. Yet when I came to your workshop and you asked us to find our true goals by focusing on what is missing in our lives, all I could think of was James. Now I'm afraid I've made a terrible mistake. And to make matters worse, now James says he doesn't want to marry me, either. I feel so terrible. I really blew it."

"Carol," I said, "let's take a closer look at your Heart's Desires.

First, let's focus on your engagement to James. There must have been reasons for ending it. What were they?"

"The main reason was the James was irresponsible," she said. "He didn't have a steady job, and I ended up paying most of our expenses. He had money at times and shared it when he did, but I just never knew what to count on. I felt like he had all the freedom and I did all the work."

"Well, that sounds like a good reason to break off an engagement. So what *do* you love about James? What is it about him that you're missing?"

"James is very passionate and exciting," Carol answered. "He's an activist and his life is full of interesting people and experiences. Compared to my boring life, James livened things up. Without him my life is really dull."

"Carol, when I teach the Principles of Creativity I emphasize the need to focus on what you *really* want. In your case, I believe James is not what you really long for. It's the excitement and creativity he brought to your life that you desire. James was just a means to an end. In order to fulfill your dream, you must consider creating that kind of excitement for yourself."

Carol turned bright red and looked embarrassed. "Sonia, I can hardly consider myself creative or passionate. I would feel silly. It's so unlike me." But she didn't sound convincing.

"Come on, Carol. Is that really true, or is it just a habit? Haven't you ever secretly wanted to get involved in something you care passionately for?"

She thought for a moment and then said, "I do care passionately for the earth. And if I were to be really honest, I'd even admit I have a talent for public speaking."

"So why don't you make that your heart's desire—developing your speaking abilities and getting involved in an organization like Greenpeace?"

Carol left with her focus redirected toward her true Heart's

Desire: a more meaningful and exciting purpose of her own. Months later I heard from her. She told me she was actively involved in earth-saving politics and had joined Toastmasters. She also said she was dating a very low-key man who was extremely supportive of her. She told me that now her life was exciting, and her relationship felt secure, a complete reversal of her exciting but unsatisfying relationship with James.

THINK BIG!

One mistake many people make in trying to identify their goals is to approach the task as if they are allowed only one goal and had better get it right! And it had better be the highest moral and spiritual goal they can think of. Such a strict and punitive approach, however, creates problems in finding what your heart really desires.

The truth is that you can and do create all the time, even if your creations aren't quite what you had in mind. The truth is also that once you learn *how* to manifest dreams, you can manifest as many as you desire. Creativity is creativity, as you will or discover as you learn the process.

Every aspect of your life is a miracle, large or small, satisfying or not. Lorraine came to realize she was blocked from identifying her *true* goals because she wasn't recognizing her obvious and very real desire for support as an authentic Heart's Desire. Carol didn't consider her desire for passion a worthy desire. In each case the focus was too limited and too lofty—both women were overlooking the practical and the necessary.

Without recognizing what we need in a practical way, we get stuck.

WHAT DO YOU WANT NOW?

My teachers taught me that authentic desires, the kind that are fueled with passion and intensity, are felt in your immediate circumstances, not in some faraway and distant future. If you don't know what you want, perhaps you are focusing too far into the future, overlooking the obvious needs and desires you have right now.

I experienced this years ago, when I struggled with my own inability to achieve my Heart's Desire. I wanted to write a book, yet at that time in my life I was trying to manage so many responsibilities that I never seemed to find the time or inspiration to begin writing. The frustration and guilt I felt over my lack of progress left me feeling very discouraged.

Applying the First Principle to my situation, I examined my goals and beliefs. Though I wanted to write a book about living intuitively, my inner voice kept saying that the timing was wrong. Being a take-charge, headstrong person, I didn't like the messages that kept surfacing in my heart. My mind said, "Patience." And it was this inner voice that ultimately commanded consideration.

I asked myself some very important goal-identifying questions:

Was I afraid?

Was I insecure?

Did I feel I wasn't qualified to write?

Was I deluding myself about my writing abilities?

Examining these questions, I had to honestly say no—my fears were not the obstacles that blocked me. It took some serious reflection and objectivity, but eventually the real reason for my procrastination came to light.

The reality of my life was that I had two small daughters, ages one and two; a house in the total disarray that comes with renovation; and a husband who was gone three days a week. The work of writing could not be a true Heart's Desire for me at *that* time, although it could remain a future goal.

My honest reflection revealed that what I really wanted was time to spend with my daughters without feeling guilty. I also wanted to get my fifteen-month-old daughter to sleep through the night, a feat I had yet to accomplish, leaving me totally exhausted most of the time. It was also my immediate Heart's Desire to bring order to my seriously disrupted house. These were the things I *was* focused on. These were the goals that were important to me, although I couldn't see it. Writing a book would only draw my focus and attention further away from my immediate desires, which is why I couldn't get started.

It was a lucid moment that taught me to approach my goals one step at a time. I couldn't reach for my dream of writing a book while my hands were full with a chaotic house and children. I couldn't reach for my dream while my heart was invested in another direction. My dream required time and patience, neither of which I had at that moment. Once I identified the proper order of things, I put my focus on my true goals and began to feel relief and progress.

If you are struggling with your Heart's Desire and are certain that it *is* what you want, be sure that you are not overlooking anything more immediately in need of your focus, attention, and care. It may well be that your intuition is simply directing you to attend to other steps that must be taken first to lay the foundation for your Heart's Desire.

If you can't identify what your heart desires, then try to identify what bugs, depresses, frustrates, aggravates, drains, irritates, or impedes you at this very moment. When you identify those things, ask yourself what you would like to have happen *instead*.

Remember that the First Principle of Creativity is that you create what you focus on. Focus is the key. Bring your own focus up front and close. Focus means sharpening your awareness on a very tight, specific area—like today, tomorrow, this week. Forget next year! Focus your awareness on you: your life, your circumstances, your health, your home, your relationships as they are today. Chances are you may be very focused on what you do not like in these areas.

Are you focusing on

1.   how much you dislike your job?
2.   how unhappy you are with your relationships?
3.   how jealous you are of someone else and what they have created?
4.   how unattractive you are?
5.   how broke you are?
6.   how lonely, misunderstood, or miserable you are?
7.   how tired, overextended, or rushed you are?
8.   how unhealthy, uncooperative, or uncomfortable your body is?
9.   how trapped, bored, or depressed you are?
10. how unfulfilled, uninspired, or unproductive you are?

If so, you are creating the miracle of these conditions even though they make you unhappy. What you must do is shift your focus to more satisfying experiences, such as

1.   working at a job you love passionately.
2.   feeling loved and appreciated.
3.   experiencing abundance.
4.   feeling your true beauty.
5.   paying your bills easily and spending your money wisely.
6.   having kinship with others.

7. asking for support without hesitation.
8. being healthy and balanced in mind, body, and soul.
9. having time to nurture yourself.
10. feeling motivated, creative, and productive.

"But how can I?" people lament. "It's not true!"

I can only share the great wisdom passed on to me by my mother: what you experience now is as of *now*. Always be willing to be surprised. Tomorrow is still being created.

TRUE GOALS VERSUS "SHOULD" GOALS

Another obstacle to uncovering your Heart's Desire is rejecting what you really would love because you were shamed or reasoned out of it—because you believe it's too grandiose to be realistic.

Michael made an appointment to see me after attending the Heart's Desire workshop. Michael had very clear goals, yet he did not feel the burning passion to create them that was necessary to bring them into being.

"I know what I want," he said, "Yet I can't get motivated."

"What do you desire?" I asked.

He answered, "I want to go to law school and get my degree."

"What else?"

"I want to make a lot of money and retire young!" he said.

"Anything else?" I asked again.

"No... Well, except one more thing. I would *love* to work on films one day when I'm rich. But that goal is unrealistic," he finished dismissively. "I need to focus on real goals."

"Do you like film?" I probed.

"I love film. It's just so hard for anyone to get a break. If I were ever rich and could get a chance to make films, it would be so exciting. But that's a long way off, if ever! I have to focus on now.

If only I could just get myself motivated. Maybe I need Prozac."

As I listened to Michael, I heard logic, resignation, and sadness, along with a huge dose of dread. He had created a plan using his reason, a plan that ignored his heart and offered substitutions. (True desire, remember, comes from the heart, not the head.)

"Michael, your voice has no energy in it when you talk about law school. Why did you choose it?" I finally asked.

"Well, I want to pay my bills. And my parents like the idea, and they are paying for school."

"What do they think of your interest in film?"

"Not much. They say it's too hard to make money in film."

"Oh, really? Are they filmmakers?"

"No..."

"Do they know anyone in film?"

"No..."

"Do *you*?"

"Yes, I know several friends pursuing film."

"And have they found work?"

"A little... but it takes time."

"So you have *logically* decided it's better to spend your time getting a law degree, right?"

"Right! Except I can't seem to get going. I've been trying to apply for two years now."

The problem with Michael was that his reason had tricked him into believing that his true goal was financially irresponsible and couldn't support him, that pursuing it would be waste of time. This belief, combined with allowing his parents to continue to be responsible for his life, totally blocked him. Yet the reality was that by not following his heart and embracing the pathway of filmmaking, Michael was indeed wasting time—two years of his time before he came to see me.

I suggested that Michael try honestly to reassess his goals and think of going to film school. I told him if it was really his Heart's Desire, he would find a way. I also suggested that he give it a chance before he drew his conclusions about the moneymaking potential in the film industry. Finally I suggested he assume financial responsibility for his dream and not look to his parents any longer. That was a scary but intensely interesting notion for him.

"Think about it and let me know what you decide," I said.

Michael did not get back to me until three and a half years later, when I received a note from him. After another year of avoiding law school, he had finally switched his goal from law to film and received a grant and other financial aid to pay for it. Michael had thrived in film school, specialized in editing, and was currently working with an advertising agency in a fairly well-paying job. He was intent on working in feature films and had already worked on three independents. He found his financial requirements were simple and easily met. Above all, he was feeling very content living his chosen dream.

If you are blocked about your desires, ask yourself whether

1. you are overlooking the obvious and immediate needs in your life.
2. you are substituting someone else's "rational" goal for your own Heart's Desire.
3. you are dismissing *true* desires as unimportant or unrealistic.

WHAT IF YOU STILL DON'T KNOW WHAT YOU WANT?

If you know exactly what you want, consider yourself lucky. You are ahead of most people. Most of us desire only from a superficial place, like a wide-eyed kid in a candy store wanting every bonbon in sight. And the unfortunate truth is that very often we do get our bonbons of desire and swallow them up in a flash, only to be left with the bellyache of disappointment.

If you can sense and feel a deeper kind of soul desire, a desire to express your creativity, to share your love, to contribute your best to the world, then you are well on your way, for that is where real happiness comes from. The Universe works in a very organized way. Thought and intention create. Thought and intention, rising up from the authentic self—your should—create peace and happiness.

If you have no idea what you want, no idea of your Heart's Desire, realize that you may be required to go through a process of elimination to discover the answer. Start by taking your attention off yourself and focus on helping someone else. Try doing volunteer work in some place that appeals to you, whether it's a library, a food bank, a hospital or a fund-raising organization. It doesn't matter. Put your left and right feet onto the wheel of life and contribute your best. In doing so, you will remember who you really are, because you will be working from your soul.

Try it for twenty-four hours, and you'll see that this works. Charity and contribution are ego blasters. They break up self-absorption and the need to be in control. They relieve you of your own heaviness and reconnect you to the world.

HERE'S A BRIGHT IDEA!

If you find yourself completely blocked and need some inspiration, another way to discover what you desire is to access your inner creative self. The way to do this is to talk to him or her directly, by name.

I named my creative inner self Bright Idea, and if you like that name, you can use it as well. Every time I feel flat, uninspired, or out of touch with what I really desire, I simply close my eyes for a moment and ask Bright Idea to help me focus on what I really need. Bright Idea has directed me to over the years to some very surprising suggestions.

For example, after an unusually long stretch of overwork, I found myself (not surprisingly) burned out and irritable with everyone. I tried to focus on what I needed to feel peaceful, but the obvious of rest and relaxation just didn't leave me satisfied. One day, while in this noxious state, I lashed out unfairly at Patrick and my children, causing a real scene. After that I decided it was time to have a talk with Bright Idea.

"Bright Idea, please help," I said. "I need some guidance. I'm irritable, drained, and don't know what I want. My family is ready to kill me, and I'm too tired to think. Please give me some direction." Then I closed my eyes and relaxed for a few moments.

Suddenly the image of a bicycle popped into my mind—I hadn't been on one in over two years. Of course! I thought. I had forgotten how much I loved to ride along the Chicago lakefront, watching the water and enjoying the people. What a bright idea!

Bright Idea can work for you, too, by accessing the creative and inspirational part of you that is overlooked and underused. By having simple heart-to-heart chat with your inner self, you directly tap into spontaneous and creative inspiration.

Get to know the Bright Idea in you, and ask him or her to help you realize exactly what you need at this time. You'll be surprised at how accommodating he or she can be.

COUNTING YOUR BLESSINGS

Another good way to get past an impasse is to count your blessings *now*. What do you love now? What part of your Heart's Desire is present in your life today? Take a break from the future. Come back to the present. Notice the fruits of the creativity you've already expressed.

Always being focused on "more, more, more" drives one to greed and frustration. Buddha said, "All misery comes from the love of material things." Remember that joy is found in creating, not in having. If you are on a materialistic path, simplify rather than amplify. See how little you need, rather than how much more you can manifest. Get back in touch with nature. As the Bible says, "Consider the lilies of the field. Solomon in all his glory was never arrayed so well. If God will bestow so much on what is in the field today, in the oven tomorrow, consider what he will do for you."

Breathe in the scent of fresh flowers. Touch trees. Put your toes in streams. Feel the soil under your feet. Come back to earth, to this moment, and feel the riches of the Universe all around you, there for your enjoyment.

YOU HAVE TO BE YOU TO FIND YOUR HEART'S DESIRE

If you can't find your Heart's Desire, maybe it's because you can't find yourself. Consider the possibility that your ability to perceive your needs may be deadened by depression, addiction, or exhaustion. If you suspect this may be true for you (much as you may hate to admit it), make it your Heart's Desire to identify the problems and seek appropriate and loving solutions. These may include a physical exam or seeking out professional counseling or an addiction recovery group.

MANIPULATION NEVER WORKS

One final block to your Heart's Desire is having the desire to manipulate, cheat, hurt, or take advantage of anyone in any way. These desires will most likely remain frustrated objectives. Remember, true desires come from the heart, the seat of the soul, your true Divine essence. It is the Divine soul in you that creates miracles, not the lesser ego mind.

If your desires are hurtful to others or lack integrity, they surely arise from a fearful or lazy ego mind and have no genuine life force behind them. You will stew and simmer in your own negativity, and you will undoubtedly suffer in mind, body, and soul. If you have harmful goals, they defile your soul and will wreak havoc on your physical and emotional life. But most important, they reflect a grave misuse of your creativity.

This point brings to mind a client I read for years ago.

One day a woman client showed up at my door wearing a red dress, red hose, red shoes, and a red jacket. She had on red earrings, and her nails were, of course, an especially bright shade of red.

The Lady in Red came to see me because she was very upset with her husband and family. She was married to a man who was, as she put it, "nice enough, but doesn't make any money." She felt he was a burden.

She also told me that she and her sisters were estranged. She said they hadn't helped her or appreciated all she had done to take care of their mother through her terminal illness. She lamented that she had suffered enormous financial stress and felt abandoned by her selfish sisters. Her Heart's Desire was to see her husband makes some "real money" and for her sisters to give her her "fair share" of their mothers' estate, since she had done all the work. In telling her story, she was sometimes sobbing so hard, she was unable to speak. Her greatest desire of all was to be appreciated.

My reading for her showed quite another story. I saw that her husband had a good job as an engineer and that *she* had been the one who decided who got what from the estate, since her mother left no will. I also saw that she had no money problems and that her focus was distorted by a materialistic attitude and anger at her sisters for long-past injuries.

When I suggested that she try to shift her focus from the material to the spiritual and that she also try family counseling, she looked at me as if I had lost my senses. She left hurriedly, cursing me for not sympathizing with her.

Several months later another woman, Louise, came for a reading. Apparently her sister had manipulated their dying mother into canceling her will. Louise was preparing to take the sister to court to divide the estate equally.

I soon realized that Louise's sister was the Lady in Red I had seen months before. Louise told me that her mother had left an estate worth ten million dollars or more, all of which Red had kept, including every last photograph. According to Louise, Red had always been competitive for their mother's attention, and until the mother had become ill, she and her mother had never gotten along. When her mother fell ill, everyone was surprised that Red moved in. Soon after, she began making it difficult for the others to visit. After he mother died, Red kept everything of her mother's away from the sisters, and now they were headed to court.

I thought it revealing that Red, in spite of being a millionaire, may as well have been bankrupt because she was spiritually unable to experience her ill-gotten abundance. Her focus was still on missing what her sisters had had for many years—their mother's attention. Ten million dollars later and still feeling cheated, she became the cheater.

Red's actions could be the subject of endless analysis, but one thing seems abundantly clear: Nothing gained in anger, jealousy, or manipulation will ultimately prove gratifying to the soul. Whatever you desire, the loving, abundant Universe wants more than anything for you to enjoy its realization. Your perspective is distorted if you believe someone else possesses what is yours and that you must wrestle or connive it away from them. The Universe has *limitless* love pouring into your soul, giving you all the power you need to create whatever you desire.

Do not be confused or distracted by the illusion that your dreams are in the hands of another. Remember, when you assume responsibility for yourself, you receive the support of the entire loving Universe. If you are envious or dishonest, know that your mental lens is out of focus and use your full powers of awareness to shift your focus back to you.

Take this time to identify your goals. Realize that any desire is worth creating if it is true, authentic, and nonmanipulative or hurtful to another. More important, think about what you do focus on, what your awareness does dwell on—because this is surely what you are creating now.

My studies in Western cabala taught me this lesson another way. I learned that we all have two incredible powers to use in our lives, and if we use them correctly, we can create whatever we want.

They are the powers of *attention* and *intention*.

ATTENTION

If we give something our *attention*, we rest our creativity on it. Wherever we focus our attention, that is also where we direct our creative energy. If we put our attention on the wrong things, they steal our energy and leave us impotent while pulling unsavory experiences into our lives. This is what happens when we use our attention to envy others or feel jealous.

If we focus on "they have what I don't," that is what we will experience. It is also what happens when we focus our attention on the worst part of what is happening to us every day or the worst that *could* happen. In doing so, we actually create and experience just that—the worst.

This is such a simple rule, yet it is the one I see most often ignored. To create your Heart's Desire you must give it your full attention.

Can you hold your attention on your Heart's Desire? If you can't, then it's probably not a true Heart's Desire, because a true Heart's Desire *will* hold your attention.

My client Mario constantly told me he wanted to be healthy; he was plagued with more physical crises than anyone I knew. He had gout, a bad back, mild arthritis, kidney stones, bunions, earaches, shingles, hives, allergies, insomnia, burstitis, and gas. Every time

I saw him he'd say, "You'll never believe what I have this week!" Mario focused all his attention (and that of anyone else who would listen) on his continuing saga of aches and pains. His whole life centered on doctors' appointments and chiropractic visits.

At one point I asked, "Are you bragging or complaining? I can't tell."

No wonder his health never improved. He was giving his illness his full attention rather than focusing on the rewards of being healthy. He was enjoying the attention his ill health provided too much to give it up.

As far as I know, Mario is still having the same health problems today, and he still doesn't believe what I told him: "You create what you put your attention on."

INTENTION

Once you focus your attention on what you want to create, you can then access your second greatest power, the power of intention. Life starts moving in the right direction when you put your attention on your Heart's Desire and then make it your *intention* to create it.

Intention is power.

Intention if ownership.

Intention is commitment.

Intention is magic.

When you work with intention, you cut away the distractions, eliminate the obstacles, and establish a connection between yourself and your dream. Intention begins to arrange your awareness so that you will notice and then seize upon all that you need to make your dream come true.

Intention is not like wishful thinking, which is abstract, vague, passive, and diffused. Intention is like an arrow flying toward a target. Intention lays claim to your creative expression and establishes the foundation of your dreams.

Scott came to the Heart's Desire workshop last winter to create the experience of finding both a soul mate and a gratifying job. During the workshop he particularly embraced the power of intention and decided right then and there that he wouldn't wish for a soul mate. Instead would *intend* to find one. Inspired by the way my husband, Patrick, and I work together, Scott further intended that his soul mate would work with him in the same compatible way.

Several months later, while attending a lecture at a local spiritual bookstore, Scott met Kim. Theirs was an instant attraction. By the time the lecture was over they had a date, and their attraction blossomed into love and partnership practically overnight. Within months they created a fast-food pretzel business together. Much to my delight, I recently learned that Scott and Kim are soon to be married.

By using the power of intention, Scott changed his Heart's Desire into reality almost immediately.

Like many people who survived the prisoner of war camps of World War II, my mother possesses enormous powers of intention, and intention was a central theme of our family life. My mother taught us never to say die. As a family of nine we never had much money, but my mom would say, "Let's intend what we need and we will have it." And we did.

My earliest recollection of this kind of manifestation was when I was eight years old. My older brother Stefan was then seventeen and thinking about going to college. My father was a salesman who supported all of us on his income, and Stefan was discouraged at the apparent lack of funds for his college tuition. I overheard him talking to my mother about his fear that he would never be able to go to the Colorado School of Mines, a prestigious engineering school in our state, because she and Dad couldn't afford it.

My mother never had (and still hadn't) any patience for someone saying "never."

"Stop it!" she said after listening for a few minutes. "I intend for you to go to the school of your dreams, and so does God. Don't worry about how. You just worry about your grades and let the Universe worry about the tuition."

Stefan, a rationalist even then and a straight A student, got angry at her refusal to face financial reality. "Be real! There's a lot of competition for scholarships, and people apply from all over the world. There's no way even *my* grades will pay for school."

Unfazed, my mother said, "Mark my words. Apply to the college anyway. You *will* go, and you will get the money you need."

Frustrated, Stefan stormed out. Wanting to go to this school, and afraid he never would be able to, he had given up before he even applied. My mother, however, did not give up. Quite the contrary—she never even considered that Stefan had a problem.

"You'll go! You will see!" she yelled after him.

Finally, giving in to her confident optimism (and her pushing him), Stefan did eventually apply to the school. In the end he was one of only ten applicants to receive a full five-year scholarship, all tuition paid. And the day Stefan came screaming through the door with the letter announcing his award, my mother only smiled and said, "As I always intended!"

Wishes and hopes are potentially weak and can be diminished, deflected, and dashed. Intentions, on the other hand, are royal and, when they rise up from the soul, will be treated royally. Circumstances will bow to them. People will honor them. Others will be inspired by them. Because true intentions are so rare, they will be treated with unusual respect.

So to begin making your dream a reality, apply the First

Principle of Creativity. *Focus* on what you want to create, give it your full *attention*, and make it your *intention* to experience it!

Now let's move on to practicing the First Principle.

PRACTICING THE FIRST PRINCIPLE

In the world of creativity, all desires are equal. There is no such thing as a "worthy" or "unworthy" desire. There are, however, *true* Heart's Desires versus "should" desires, which are really an attempt to live up to other people's notions of what is desirable. These Principles will manifest only true Heart's Desires. They will support only what comes from your heart and not from guilt or fear.

RANK YOUR DESIRES IN ORDER OF PRIORITY

In order to identify your true Heart's Desires—as they exist *now*—rank them according to how important they are to you. Number them one through ten.

___ HEALTH AND BODY

___ FINANCES

___ RELATIONSHIPS

___ HOME

___ WORK

___ CREATIVE EXPRESSION

___ TRAVEL/ADVENTURE

___ POSSESSIONS

___ SPIRITUAL

___ SPECIAL INTENTION

FOCUSING ON YOUR HEART'S DESIRE

Create a space to write down exactly what you *do* want to create *now*. Start with your needs and desires.

1.   HEALTH AND BODY. This means the sphere of physical health and well-being, including weight loss or gain, beauty, exercise, sport, and recovery from illness.

....

....

....

2.   FINANCES. This includes the sphere of income, savings, debt payoff, and money for purchases, adventures, and indulgences.

....

....

....

3.   RELATIONSHIPS. This includes the sphere of love, romance, marriage, divorce, children, parents, relatives, friends, neighbors, partners, and pets.

....

....

4.   HOME. This includes buying, selling, renting, remodeling, building, moving, acquiring roommates, decorating, and designing where you live.

....

....

....

5.   WORK. This includes where you want to work, what you want
to do, how much you want it to pay, whom you want to work with, the
environment you want to work in, the rewards you want to receive,
the amount of independence you want, and the contribution to the
world you want to make.

....

....

....

6.   CREATIVE EXPRESSION. This includes singing, dancing, painting,
writing, healing, intuiting, inventing, building, designing, photographing,
acting, producing, filming, cooking, gardening, sculpting.

....

....

....

7.   TRAVEL/ADVENTURE. This includes travel, sports, recreation,
retreat, world exploration, psychic exploration, and new experiences
of every kind.

....

....

....

8.   POSSESSIONS. This includes any and all physical objects
and property that may make your daily life more joyous, more
pleasurable, more comfortable, more practical, and more fun.

....

....

9.   SPIRITUAL. This includes the sphere of personal discovery, healing old wounds, recovering personal power, expanding intuitive awareness, discovering new dimensions, remembering your true spiritual identity.

....

....

....

10.   SPECIAL INTENTION. This includes anything not covered above.

....

....

....

Now review your desire lists and identify three desires you want to concentrate on creating first. Use the meditation following to help you select them. You can focus more effectively by working on only a few desires at a time. Every time you realize a dream, you can go back to your list to work on another one. When you have selected three desires, fill in the following:

I,_____, use the full power of my intention and attention to create the following desires now:

1.   ....

2.   ....

3.   ....

MEDITATION

This is the first meditation in a series, one for each chapter of this book, designed to enhance your practice of the Principles. It is very helpful to work daily with the meditation for the Principle you are currently working on.

You might like to read the meditations into a sound recorder or have them read to you by someone you feel comfortable with. As you read aloud, pause at the end of each paragraph to allow yourself to form the images fully in your mind.

Find a comfortable spot where you can sit quietly without being interrupted for at least ten minutes.

Close your eyes and pay attention to your breath as it enters and then leaves your body.

Once you are in a calm, balanced, physical and emotional state, ask your Higher Self, "What is it that I desire now?"

Gently allow your Higher Self to answer this question. Do not block, judge, or censor the answer. Simply accept whatever comes.

Continue breathing easily for a few minutes. Make it your intention to focus on creating this dream.

Then, when you are ready, slowly open your eyes.

PRINCIPLE NUMBER TWO

Gain the Support of Your Subconscious Mind

Once you focus on what you intend to create, you naturally move on to the Second Principle of Creativity—gaining the support of your subconscious mind.

The Second Principle teaches that what you consciously desires and what you subconsciously believe about that desire must be *in agreement* for you to succeed. If you hold your attention on a conscious desire, but subconsciously harbor beliefs that are in conflict with your goal, you are going to come to a creative impasse.

Let me illustrate with a story about a client of mine named Susan.

When Susan first came to see me for an intuitive reading, she was very frustrated in her job as a manager for a large corporation. Whenever she wanted to make a decision, Susan was obliged to get the approval of two bosses who were far more conservative and, she felt, less effective in managing people than she was. Susan was fed up!

For well over six months Susan had been planning to leave her job and create her own management training firm. She had even met other women who had done what she dreamed of doing and were thriving both creatively and financially. These women accepted and treated Susan as one of their own. As Susan put it, "I've been invited to sit at their table and break bread, and it feels right."

Yet in spite of being clearly focused on her goal and having both the background and support to follow through, when it came right down to it, Susan had a death grip on her job. She explained that each time she moved toward actually saying "I quit!" a dark shadowy feeling of doom overcame her. She was unable to focus at work, irritable with her husband and son, and embarrassed to talk to the women who encouraged her. Susan was frozen into immobility, and she was angry.

Exasperated, she asked, "*What* is my problem?!"

I suggested we look for her blocks. Consciously Susan was applying the creative Principle of focus very well and was ready to emancipate and go for her dream, but I could tell that subconsciously, conflicting beliefs were holding her back.

Susan came from a strict Dutch working-class family and had a rigid Dutch Reform upbringing. In this environment she had been taught that wanting financial success was greedy, and anyone who had money was a self-indulgent sinner. Also, despite the fact that her husband was happy she had a job, she had subconsciously accepted the notion that as a female she should stay home, raise kids, and take the lead from her husband.

Susan had long ago consciously left the oppressive environment of her childhood and set up her own life, married, and had a child, but subconsciously these old messages had sunk in and were still operating. Now these long-forgotten attitudes broke through like the Creature from the Black Lagoon, blocking her from her dream. She felt like a bad girl, wanting more than she should ask for and expecting to be punished.

Until Susan recognized these sabotaging beliefs and could replace them with more balanced and supportive ones, she was stuck. She was spinning her creative wheels in the muck of such oppressive attitudes. In order to move out of this impasse, Susan needed to reconcile these learned beliefs of submission with her present and conscious creative desire to work for herself.

When Susan examined them consciously, she agreed that she had conflicts about her Heart's Desire and negative beliefs about success that were indeed holding her back.

This problem is not unique to Susan. It can be found at the root of every frustrated artist, every would-be actor, every closet writer, every overextended caretaker, every potential entrepreneur, and every member of the Lonely Hearts Club. Beliefs, if contrary to what we desire, stop our creative expression dead, because *we create what we believe!* That is the Second Principle of Creativity.

After our discussion, Susan decided, at age forty-two, to change her beliefs and gain the support of her subconscious mind. She no longer wanted to feel like a little child wanting the approval she had never gotten in her critical home environment. She wanted to become more self-approving. She read spiritual books that inspired her, such as *Creative Visualization* and *The Artist's Way*, and she joined Unity, a progressive church that professed more loving values. She even made a doll that looked like her so she could champion herself symbolically with creative and empowering approval, a suggestion taken from *The Artist's Way*.

Eventually Susan did quit her job to start her own firm. Slowly but surely she is now advancing in the entrepreneurial world, feeling very satisfied with her creative freedom. An added bonus was the fact that once she took the plunge, her parents proved to be the most supportive of all. As her beliefs changed, so did theirs. They now openly say how proud they are of her courage in working for herself, and they admire her success.

If you are stuck like Susan, take heart. There are many ways to redirect your subconscious mind and continue to move toward your desire. The most powerful way of all is to talk directly to your subconscious and tell it what you have *decided* to create.

One thing I have learned about the subconscious mind is that it is a "yes machine." All it can say is "yes"; it can't argue or disagree. Therefore, if you say to yourself, "I want to succeed," your subconscious mind will say, "Yes, I want to succeed." If you then say, "Success is sinful," your subconscious mind will say, "Yes, success is sinful." And if you keep giving it mixed messages, you will find yourself going in circles. The subconscious mind will cooperate with every direction you give it. If you give it directions that agree with your dreams, you'll stop going in circles and begin to move ahead.

The bottom line is that you must get your subconscious mind to accept and believe in your dreams in order to create them in your life. Once it does, look out—you are on your way!

My mom told me a story about the creative power of belief.

She married my father as a young Romanian war bride and came to America when she was only sixteen. Not speaking English very well, she learned as she went along.

One evening shortly after they arrived, my father took her dancing at an outdoor summer garden. After several fast dances, she asked him to get her something to drink. Moments later my father retuned with a drink in a beautiful tall glass with cherries and a little paper umbrella.

"Here's your cocktail," he told her.

My mother recognized the word "cocktail" and was surprised that my dad had brought her an alcoholic drink, but since it was a special occasion, why not? She tasted the drink. It was delicious. She drank it down in a flash, and they were off twirling on the dance floor. Feeling the effects of the drink, my mother really let loose. She was swooping, spinning, and having a great time, feeling suddenly liberated from all inhibition.

Soon she had worked up another thirst, and she asked for

another drink. Another cocktail was delivered, and she practically inhaled it. After that she was raring to go. Off to the dance floor once again, this time singing and twirling as she went. She was having the time of her life, though feeling slightly woozy.

All the dancing required one more drink. When it was brought she downed it immediately and hit the dance floor again. After a few moments she was so dizzy that she fell over. My dad caught her and dragged her to a chair.

"What is the matter with you?" he asked, both concerned and perplexed.

"You must be kidding! she said. "What do you think is the matter? Those cocktails made me drunk!"

My dad burst out laughing. "How? Those cocktails didn't have any alcohol in them. They were *kiddie* cocktails!"

"Oh, really?" she said, instantly sober.

My mom and dad laughed all the way home!

GETTING YOUR SUBCONSCIOUS MIND TO SUPPORT YOU

Your beliefs create the landscape of your experience by imprinting the subconscious mind with directives. Each belief you accept is embraced by the subconscious mind as a command, which the subconscious then sets about following.

In my workshops I explain to my students that the subconscious mind is very receptive and willing to deliver back to you whatever you tell it to do. It takes orders much like the counterperson at the fast-food drive-through: You drive up. You order what you want. Your subconscious mind, taking the order, records what you tell it and then proceeds to deliver it back to you.

It doesn't argue. It doesn't change the order. It doesn't talk you out of it. All it says I, "Yes. Yes. Yes." Then it tries to fill your order.

Now imagine that you are driving up to the Heart's Desire drive-through window. Waiting there is your very receptive and accommodating subconscious mind.

Subconscious You: *"Yes? What would you like?"*
Conscious You: *"I would like someone to love me."*
Subconscious You: *"Okay. Anything else?"*
Conscious You: *"But that'll never happen. I'm too old."*
Subconscious You: *"Okay. Anything else?"*
Conscious You: *"If I ever did find someone, how would he put up with all my idiosyncrasies?"*
Subconscious You: *"Okay. Is that all?"*
Conscious You: *"I find it hard to believe anyone could really understand and love me."*
Subconscious You: *"Yes. Anything else?"*
Conscious You: *"I really can't count on meeting someone. I'd better put the idea out of my mind so I won't be disappointed."*
Subconscious You: *"Okay. Is that all?"*
Conscious You: *"Yes, that's all."*

So the subconscious you prepares to give you the experience you asked for. Is it any wonder that what is delivered is the *wanting* but not *receiving* of love?

Now do you see how the subconscious mind works? It's not that complicated. It is simply a "yes machine." It is not discriminating or discerning. And it embraces every directive you give it. If you give it conflicting directives, it has no choice but to produce vague, unsatisfactory outcomes.

And the more conflicting the messages, the more the subconscious mind will filter through the input and latch onto those directives it has repeatedly received from you.

* * *

One example of this is the difference between my driving experiences and my husband's. Patrick believes that there are a lot of bad, rude drivers in the world, always butting in, cutting him off, and basically behaving like jerks. He especially believes this to be true of those who drive sleek luxury cars.

In keeping with the Second Principle, every time Patrick is driving, only minutes after starting out, we inevitably experience a Road Warrior encounter with some luxury-car-driving rude dude who displays the driving etiquette of a moron.

On one outing we had several white knuckle encounters with another driving boor. Patrick turned on National Public Radio to soothe his nerves, only to hear one writer's essay on the rude manners of luxury car owners on the road.

"See!" Patrick glared at me, vindicated. "I'm not the only one who thinks so!"

I just laughed and tightened my seat belt.

My own driving experiences, on the other hand, are very uneventful. I harbor no negative beliefs about other drivers, and consequently I always seem to encounter the nice guy who gives me a wave to go first or pulls out from the parking spot just as I am searching desperately for one. In fact, I have great driving luck.

It infuriates Patrick when I disagree with him over our driving experiences, mostly because we are both right about what happens on the road. It is, after all, our beliefs that write the scripts of what happens.

THE SUBCONSCIOUS MIND GIVES YOU WHAT YOU DWELL ON

In other words, your subconscious mind produces best what you dwell on. That's why you especially end up experiencing exactly what you worry about. Worry is a potent way of dwelling on something. The subconscious mind isn't trying to sabotage you. It is simply giving you its very best expression of what you impress upon it with your powers of attention and focus.

Another way to view the subconscious mind is to see it as a one-way street. It will take you the way you point it.

Knowing this is the key to programming your subconscious mind with beliefs and directives that agree with your Heart's Desire.

If you want to go in the direction of love, dwell on successful examples of love. If you want to move in the direction of health, well on pleasing images of balance and health. If you want prosperity, dwell on becoming prosperous. The same goes for freedom, for support, for opportunity, or for whatever you desire.

Focus your attention on these ideas until you believe they are waiting for you. Your subconscious mind will deliver experiences of success just as eagerly as it will disappointment. It will and can deliver only what you consciously order it to deliver.

WHAT DO YOU BELIEVE?

One way to identify your beliefs is to contemplate your Heart's Desire and ask yourself what might happen if you actually *did* manifest such a dream.

Do you uncover any anxieties or fears while doing this? Do you worry that you may be asking too much? Do you wonder how you will be responsible for your dream? Do you imagine your wish fulfilled might cause another injury or pain? Do you feel unworthy to realize such a dream? Does bringing change into your life make you nervous in any way?

Jerry, a student who took my first Heart's Desire workshop twelve years ago, put it best. He said, "In other words the Second Principle is, How good can you stand it? That's as good as it gets."

Jerry was right.

If your beliefs are contrary to your Heart's Desire, are you willing to trade them for more supportive ones? Surprisingly, many people are not.

* * *

I had a client named Joslyn who was being treated for ovarian cancer. It was her Heart's Desire to be cured, which brought her to me.

When I did a reading for her, I saw that she believed quite strongly that she must take care of everyone in every way before she attended to her own needs. This belief was further amplified by the fact that she had married a successful businessman who wanted a stay-at-home, fifties kind of housewife and mother.

Feeling guilty about not earning money, and eager to fulfill her husband's idea of what a wife should be, Joslyn exhausted herself by cooking, cleaning, carpooling, volunteering at the school and the children's hospital, and looking after her husband's mother, who lived in a nursing home. This schedule was so oppressive and exhausting that she had no avenues for self-expression. Her immune system was under attack, and she developed cancer.

I suggested she stop this extensive and endless caretaking and explore some more personally fulfilling activities as a supportive way to help herself revive and boost her healing potential.

"How can I?" she asked incredulously. "I am a mother! I have *children!* People *need me.* I can't stop."

Her reaction revealed a deeply committed belief that her worth, her work, and her responsibility lay in putting others before herself. Any suggestion to the contrary was flat-out rejected. If she wasn't a caretaker, she might not be anybody, a prospect far worse to consider than illness. Her belief was that self-care was out of the question and that doctors, not her, were in charge of her health and whether she lived or died.

"I just want to find the right doctor," she said, "so he can cure me."

Joslyn did not stop giving. She continued willfully sacrificing herself for others at a breakneck pace, and after a four-year ordeal, she died at the age of forty-three.

Could things have been different had she changed her beliefs? I believe so.

SO HOW DO I GET OUT OF MY OWN WAY?

The secret to getting out of your own way is in knowing how to impress the subconscious mind in a way that works, and the good news is that there are many ways to do this.

One way to gain subconscious support is to reorient your desire. Change your desire from simply accomplishing an outcome to actually making a contribution to the world.

For example, Roxy, a country-western singer, came to me for a consultation because she was having great difficulty practicing Principle Number Two. "The truth is, Sonia, that even though my desire is to be a successful performer, I simple *cannot* believe that it will ever happen to me," she confessed.

"Well, Roxy," I answered, "before you decide what is possible, let's examine your desire a little closer. What exactly does being successful mean to you?"

"That's easy," she replied. "It means making a lot of money."

"Is that *all* it means to you?" I asked.

She reflected a moment and said, "I suppose it also means that people will enjoy my music."

"In other words, success means that your singing has value and brings a positive experience to others."

"Yes, I guess it does mean that," she admitted.

"Perhaps, then, it will be easier to believe in your dream if you focus on the value your dream will bring to the world instead of focusing exclusively on your personal gain."

"I see what you mean," said Roxy. "When you put it that way, it is easier for me to believe in my heart's desire."

Roxy decided to reorient her focus from one of gaining approval as a singer to one of contributing her talents to the world and found her energy quickly freed up to move on to Principle Number Three.

This simple reorientation of your focus works wonders whenever you have difficulty believing in your dream. If you desire love, believe in the value of sharing your loving energy with someone who will benefit from it. If you desire a new job, believe in the value your unique talent will contribute to the company that hires you. If you want a face-lift, believe in the value of personally beautifying the environment. In other words, focus on believing in the value your desire will bring those around you. When you do this, you tap into your true purpose and bypass all old subconscious beliefs to the contrary. When you create from a desire to contribute, your subconscious mind cooperates completely. This is the *best* way to get out of your own way and get on with your dream.

Affirmations are another way to gain the support of your subconscious mind. The subconscious mind accepts best what it hears over and over. Simple statements redirect the subconscious mind best.

For example, ten years ago my husband, Patrick, quit smoking by using the simple affirmation "I prefer health," followed by a deep breath, every time he felt the impulse to light a cigarette. This affirmation eliminated his desire to smoke in a few days, and he's been smoke-free ever since.

One of my favorite affirmations is taken from the comedian Billy Crystal. As his character Fernando says, "You look *mah*velous!" Every morning when I look in the mirror I say this affirmation out loud. It makes me laugh but, sure enough, I immediately feel better about myself. My friend Monty's favorite affirmation is "Life is a symphony and I love the music." He also has a spring in his step and a bright smile on his face whenever I see him.

If you desire love, try the affirmation "I love being loved." Of if you desire prosperity, try "The universe is very generous to me."

Another delightful way to affirm new directions is to create a personal song or mantra. One of my clients, in the midst of great personal difficulties, invented a little ditty that went like this:

Through divine grace
I move into my rightful place
I am free of old drama
I don't need the trauma…

Of course it's silly, but it worked. She sang her subconscious into compliance and began to feel able to move on.

Another way to gain subconscious support is to find what my friend Julia Cameron, author of *The Artist's Way*, calls "believing mirrors." In other words, it will be much easier to believe in your dreams if you surround yourself with safe and enthusiastic people who believe in you even while you struggle. Principle Number Two is called "Gain the *Support* of Your Subconscious Mind." But it could also be called "Gain Support." So many of us still have open wounds from not receiving the support we needed as children, and we find ourselves crippled by the disbelief of these nonsupportive ghosts from our past. By replacing such phantom voices with live, enthusiastic ones in the present, your subconscious mind will override outworn input and begin to embrace new and more positive influences, thereby getting on with the task of making these dreams real. You can find such support in Artist's Way study groups, private therapy, Twelve Step groups, spiritual communities, and weekend workshops. You can also find support in a loving and creative teacher or with true friends and lovers. The truth is that we do a far better job believing in ourselves when supported by loving forces than we do all alone.

Prayer is still another way to gain subconscious support. Here is a simple prayer for subconscious direction:

"I offer my dreams as a source of love to the world. In their
fulfillment I will bring a message of light to all that I touch."

This prayer, if repeated daily, is a powerful statement to the subconscious mind. After all, if you are working for God, what is going to stop you? Even the subconscious complies quickly when God is on the job.

There are many ways to redirect your subconscious mind and create beliefs that will continue to move you toward your desires. But the most powerful way of all is to tell your mind to follow your *decisions*. A decision is a strong statement to your subconscious mind. Decision is focus in action. Decision is owning your dream. It is directing your full attention down the one-way street called Your Heart's Desire. So make it your decision to see the value in your desire, affirm its reality, actively seek support, and offer your dreams to the betterment of the planet through prayer.

As Ralph Blum says in *The Book of Runes*, "There is only one power in the Universe, and that is the power of decision. All else follows."

PRACTICING THE SECOND PRINCIPLE

WHAT YOU ALREADY BELIEVE

Create a space to write down all beliefs you have, good or bad, regarding your dreams. Don't censor, just reflect, and answer as honestly as possible.

I believe success is ....

....

I believe money is ....

....

I believe health is ....

....

I believe adventure is ....

....

I believe creativity is ....

....

I believe spiritual peace is ....

....

I believe love is ....

....

What I want to believe about my Heart's Desire now is ....

....

YOUR SONG

Write a song or mantra for your new beliefs. (I know this feels silly, but it's fun, and it works! Go ahead.)

NEGATIVE BELIEF BUSTER RITUAL

The subconscious mind responds well to ritual. When you do this cleansing ritual, try burning incense, lighting candles, ringing bells, or playing special music—the more passionate, the better.

First, write down all the negative beliefs that you have that are contrary to your dream.

....

....

....

....

Next, tell your subconscious mind (out loud!):

> *Now hear this! These negative beliefs are no longer in charge.*
> *I burn and release them from my subconscious memory. I no*

longer allow them to influence me in any way. I replace them with my new, empowering beliefs. I replace them with the truth about my Divine essence!

Then burn the old beliefs, flush the ashes down the toilet, and wash your hands.

ONE WAY TO YOUR HEART'S DESIRE

Write down new beliefs on cutout one-way traffic signs, like this:

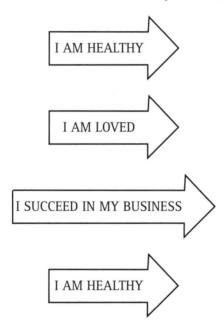

Post them in strategic places. For example, place I AM PROSPEROUS in your wallet, I AM BEAUTIFUL on the mirror in the bathroom, I LOOK MARVELOUS in your closet, I SUCCEED IN BUSINESS in your desk drawer. The whole idea here is to create, so be creative, and use your sense of humor. One client put I AM SEXY in her underwear drawer! Doing this gets right to the center of your subconscious mind and really does support your spirit.

HEART-TO-HEART WITH YOUR SUBCONSCIOUS

Write down your Heart's Desire(s), then fill in the following chart:

MY HEART'S DESIRE	
HOW WILL I SEE MYSELF WHEN I REALIZE MY DREAM?	
HOW WILL OTHERS SEE ME WHEN I REALIZE MY DREAM?	
WHAT POSSIBLE NEGATIVITY MAY I ENCOUNTER IF I REALIZE MY DREAM?	
HOW WILL MY ENVIRONMENT CHANGE IF I REALIZE MY DREAM?	
HOW WILL MY RELATIONSHIPS CHANGE IF I REALIZE MY DREAM?	

WHAT AM I AFRAID OF IF I REALIZE MY DREAM?	
WHAT REWARDS DO I HOPE TO EXPERIENCE IF I REALIZE MY DREAM?	

MEDITATION

Find a comfortable spot where you can sit quietly without being interrupted for at least fifteen minutes.

Close your eyes and pay attention to your breath as it enters and then leaves your body.

Focus your full attention on your Heart's Desire and notice and mental distractions that come up in your thoughts.

As you continue to breathe and focus on your dream, take a look at what pulls your attention away. Look at these distractions in a nonjudgmental way and notice whether they are fears, worries, other people's opinions, or beliefs that you have outgrown. As you continue breathing, envision that these distractions are being pulled out of your consciousness by gravity and swallowed into the earth.

Imagine your conscious and unconscious mind coming together to form a single focus, like a needle on a compass, pointing directly toward your dream. As you do this, imagine your body, mind, and spirit filling with Divine grace.

As you end this meditation, make a conscious choice *to be receptive to experiencing your dream with each breath you take from this moment forward.*

When you are ready, slowly open your eyes.

REVIEW

Finally, answer one more question: Do you *believe* you are ready to realize your dream? If the answer is yes, go on to the next Principle.

If the answer is no, return to Principle Number One and start again.

Imagine Your Heart's Desire

Gaining the support of your subconscious mind will carry you to the threshold of the Third Principle of Creativity, which teaches that what you desire is born into the world through your imagination.

Imagination will accept a true Heart's Desire and give it the breath of life. It is the realm where a dream takes on color, sound, size, and movement. Imagination is like a fertile garden, accepting your desires and dreams as soil in which you have planted seeds. These seeds become ideas that, when gently cultivated, burst into full bloom.

Imagination is the womb of your life. It is the place where your desires are nurtured and protected, where they are kept safe while they grow and develop. Your imagination expands your dreams until they can no longer be contained and must insist themselves into being. Imagination is the birthplace of all possibility.

Often my teacher Charlie would say, "Look around, Sonia. What do you see?"

"Well," I would answer, observing his living room, "I see furniture, books, rugs, a fireplace..."

"What you really see is not only that!" he'd say. "You see imagination, Sonia. Wonderful, marvelous, ingenious imagination! For example, notice the carvings on the arms and the ornate needlepoint work on the rocking chair. Notice the intricate patterns and bright colors in the Oriental rug. Notice the fireplace façade is made of marble and mantel is carved in burly oak. Every detail in this room, including the room itself, is a direct example of someone's imaginings."

And I realized it was true. Everything ever invented was first imagined in great details. My mom used to say, "You cannot experience what you cannot imagine... yet you always experience what you *do* imagine." And my teacher Dr. Tully taught me that if I ever wanted anything, I needed to imagine it into being first.

"Real imagination," he taught me, "involved all of your senses and all of your emotions. Real imagination is often best engaged by people when they fear something. Many people are very good at this. They fear an outcome so strongly that their senses and emotions get going and bring their dreaded imaginings right to them."

In my own practice I have even noticed in some of my clients a tendency to *intentionally* imagine the worst-case scenario instead of their Heart's Desire. This seems to be a convoluted way of protecting themselves from experiencing the pain of disappointment. Oddly, it is as though they believe fearing the worst at the outset will prevent letdowns later on. Little do they know that this actually *doubles* their pain—first anticipating disappointment, then by attracting it. Maybe that's what Jesus meant when he said, "And their fears shall come upon them."

The whole idea of Principle Number Three is just the opposite: to use the full power of imagination to evoke an internal experience of what you really want. When you deeply imagine your true Heart's Desire, you will be amazed at how eagerly your full sensory self cooperates.

As a matter of fact, you can tell whether something is a true Heart's Desires by whether or not you are able to imagine it clearly. Check and see.

Can you envision your Heart's Desire? Can you touch it in your mind? What does it look like? What does it feel, sound, smell like? Can you taste it? If you can imagine your Heart's Desire in this way, you are creating a Heart's Desire imagination blueprint. When you create such a blueprint, it becomes the door for these dreams to enter your life.

Let me tell you a story of how my own imagination whisked me to my dream of living in the South of France.

All my life I had fantasized about living in the South of France, and these imaginings conjured up the most profoundly warm feelings deep within my soul. The more I imagined going there, the more compelled I was to do it. My first attempt at realizing my dream was to become a flight attendant. But, alas, my job took me to cities like Cleveland and Pittsburgh, and I found myself no close to France than I had been before!

One day I had to wait for several hours in the Detroit airport before making the connection to work my next flight. As I sat waiting in the crew lounge, I struck up a conversation with a fellow flight attendant named Richard who also had a few hours to pass. We talked about work at first, but eventually our conversation turned to more personal matters. I told him how frustrated I was with my job and how my real ambition was to move to southern France.

To my surprise, Richard said, "It's lovely, I did just that myself."

"You lived in France?" I asked, feeling both jealous and intrigued.

"Yes," he said. "Eight years ago. I lived in a town called Aix-en-Provence and had a fantastic experience."

I started to ask him to suggest how I could do the same, but he looked at his watch and noticed he had to get to his flight. He jotted something down on a piece of paper, saying, "It's easier than you think once you decide to go. That's the hard part."

Handing me the paper, he said, "Here's the name of the family

I lived with. If you ever do get there, perhaps they can be of help. Good luck."

The piece of paper was the first solid connection to my dream. I had never even heard of Aix-en-Provence, but judging by Richard's description, I thought it sounded like the perfect destination. Right then and there *I* decided that somehow I was going.

With that decision, my imagination kicked into full sensory operation. I imagined renting a small room in "Aix," as Richard referred to it, and living there in grand Bohemian fashion. I imagined the scent of the lavender he said grew there filling my nostrils as I wandered in the fields surrounding the town. I imagined tasting the wonderful cheeses, drinking the wine, and crunching on baguettes. I imagined speaking impeccable French with handsome men and strolling down the Cours Mirabeau, the town version of the Champs-Élysées that Richard had described.

My musings moved me. I read French-language books, listened to Edith Piaf records, and pored over Frommer's *France on Twenty Dollars a Day*. I knew I had to go, but I didn't want to go alone. Whom could I go with?

I decided to convince my friend Heidi, a malcontent cocktail waitress, to join me.

"How exciting!" she said. "Sounds great. I wish I could."

The minute she said that, I mobilized my efforts completely to get her to say yes. I used the same technique Richard had on me.

I said, "Heidi, it's easy once you decide."

She balked. "Where would we stay?" she said with a nervous laugh. I could see she was beginning to consider the offer.

I paused. This was moment to make or break her decision. My imagination took over completely.

Thinking of the names on Richard's paper, I said, "It's no problem. I have friends we can stay with." Even though I couldn't explain why, I felt I was telling the truth. I was describing what I intuitively and imaginatively felt would be so.

"What the heck," Heidi finally said, snared. "Let's go for it."

Our course was set. Two months later I received a six-month leave from my job, Heidi quit hers, and we were off.

We were high on a romantic, adventurous whirlwind—until, jet-lagged and anxious, we arrived in Paris, where our imaginings collided with reality. Paris was expensive, impersonal, and overwhelming. We decided to leave after only one day.

"To the south, where the good life is!" we chanted, boarding the express train at the Gare de Lyon, glad to get out of town. Halfway between Lyon and Marseilles, Heidi, now suffering serious culture shock and jet lag, asked me about my "friends."

Oh my. I drew in a deep breath.

"Heidi, about our friends... There's one thing I haven't mentioned. I haven't met them yet. I just have their names on a piece of paper given to me by someone who knows them. But don't worry. I'm sure they will be as wonderful and welcoming as I imagine them to be."

She was horrified to hear they weren't expecting us.

Clinging to my imaginings the rest of the way (and not wanting to hear about hers at the moment), I moved to the other side of the railroad car and looked for an inexpensive hotel in my Michelin guide. We arrived in Marseilles at midnight, and our taxi took us to the Hotel Martini, my one-star choice.

To our dismay, the Martini was a seedy flophouse two blocks from the train station. Starving and disgusted by the hotel, we decided to put up with it for one night and went looking for a place to eat.

The area surrounding the hotel was as creepy as the hotel itself. It was bleak and deserted for the most part, except for an occasional smoky, dim bar. Our prospects for dinner looked slim. Motivated by intense hunger, however, we continued to hunt for a café. A few blocks later we heard loud, angry voices ahead. As we rounded a corner we came upon a group of street thugs engaged in a brawl.

We startled them and Heidi let out a scream. They started toward us and we spun on our heels, scared out of our minds. As we raced around the corner back toward the hotel, we were suddenly in the headlights of a police paddy wagon. Three cops jumped out.

"Arrêtez-vous!" they shouted, guns pointing at us.

I couldn't believe what was happening. We had been in Marseilles only thirty minutes, and now we were being mistaken for druggies, prostitutes, or worse and thrown into the back of a police paddy wagon! Not quite what I had imagined, but what an adventure.

Heidi was in shock. I must have been, too, because I started laughing. The whole experience had become too weird by now for even *my* imagination. Two of the cops got into the back of the wagon with us while the other got into the cab and began to drive.

Heidi demanded that I explain who we were, that we were lost and hungry and scared and...

I knew I couldn't manage all that with my rusty French, but after a few scary minutes I managed to say, *"Nous sommes perdues!"* (We are lost.)

The cops were agitated and asked us for our passports. We handed them over and held our breath. They scrutinized them very carefully.

Finally one of them smiled and said, "First time here, eh?"

"Oui, oui!" we answered, our heads bobbing like apples in a bucket of water.

"Where you stay?"

When I said, "Hotel Martini," they rolled their eyes, and one cop pantomimed having his throat slit.

"Cripes!" said Heidi. "Now what?"

The cops continued talking among themselves for a few minutes. Finally one said, "You need good room, yes?"

He took pity on us. He whispered back and forth heatedly with the two other cops, then said, "No worry. I help. *Grand-mère* room, in Aix. We go you."

In another thirty minutes we had picked up our bags from the flophouse and were whisked to the safety of a beautiful country home just outside the small town of Aix, our original destination! The policeman's grandmother got up, greeted us, and made us a meal of salami, baguettes, cheese, and fresh fruit. She then led us to a wonderful room that I later discovered overlooked a hillside of lavender, just as I had imagined.

"See, Heidi?" I said, finally drifting to sleep in my cozy bed after our exhausting thirty-six hour ordeal. "I told you we had friends in the South of France!"

This experience showed me the miraculous power of the imagination. When you really imagine your Heart's Desire, a life force stirs deep within and burns in your soul. It is an energy that takes over your thoughts, takes over your emotions, and moves into your life like a garden bursting into bloom. And it attracts its real-life counterparts into your path!

Imagination defines. Imagination invents. Imagination gives the Heart's Desire a conduit into the world. If your desire is true and your beliefs support it, then your imagination will embrace your desire into its rich, fertile soil and begin to give it life.

DOES YOUR IMAGINATION BELONG TO YOU?

Imagination creates your life. It governs your choices. It dictates your likes and dislikes. It moves your feet. It fills your attention. It paints the world you live in. It is your most magnificent tool, yet many people have allowed their imaginations to be stolen away, only to be replaced with cheap substitutes.

Stop yourself if your imagination is overdosing on the secondhand drama and regurgitated filler of daytime TV, the mental chewing gum of CNN, or the mindless dribble of sitcom America. Protect yourself from soul-deadening images of violence, pain, and suffering as entertainment. Keep a vigilant guard over who governs what you imagine. People surrender their creativity to these perverted and plastic versions of reality to such a degree that they actually believe those images are the real world.

Notice how TV no longer imitates people; rather, people are now imitating TV or the movies. Many people have long ago stopped imagining from the deep, desirous, soulful place they knew as children. Instead they project other people's images onto their mental screen. They let their images go as far as the person next to them has gone, and no farther. This domino effect has diminished potentially inventive minds to mere imitators.

The things so many people copy are depressing, disappointing, deadening images of failure, pain, and sorrow. We follow the leader, think what we are told to think, and accept others' opinions as fact. In so doing, we lose real creative power.

When I worked as a flight attendant I was faced with daily doses of gloom and doom as my airline, like all the others, went through the many aches and pains of deregulation. In 1985 I finally chose to bow out and devote myself full-time to intuitive counseling and spiritual teaching. Yet I had many dear friends (and two family members) who still worked for the airline. Nearly every day one of these friends would call, near tears, and say something like "I heard the airline is going to close their doors next week! How can I pay my bills if that happens?" Or "It's over. I'm going to be unemployed any day now!"

The anxiety these people felt rippled through the terminals like the plague. Everyone was telling everyone else that the end was near. I recall even speaking at one point to a newspaper reporter who told me he had already written the story of the airline's shutdown.

"It's inevitable," he said. "It's a fact waiting to happen."

That was eleven years ago. As I write this, the planes are still flying. Also as I write this, some people are still worried sick, no matter that eleven years later business continues as always and they still have their jobs. Even though some airlines did shut down, new ones formed in their place and many flight attendants and pilots found jobs. In other words, change doesn't have to mean the end. It means only that it's time for something new.

During all of this turmoil I also noticed a tendency on the part of certain people to fan the flames of negativity, gossiping like clucking chickens over what they had heard as if it were true, enjoying the ensuing upset and drama it stirred up. These were usually people who had no real sense of life and love, so they created images to tear down that sense in others.

Be on guard for this. Don't let gossip be the basis of your reality. Any time you hear someone say "I heard..." take it as your cue to walk away. Know that whatever happens, you can deal with it.

From now on, let your own imagination be the *original* scriptwriter of your experience. Authentic imagination has the courage to be original. It turns inward. It feels the soul's inspiration, and the images come from God.

Real imagination accepts no limitations. It challenges the boundaries of conventional wisdom. And those who use this magnificent power are having the best time doing it!

Think about it. Someone tapped into authentic imagination and courageously imagined flying. Now we can go farther than Mars. Another courageously imagined talking to someone across the country, and now we can talk to one another across the globe, face-to-face, via computer screen images. Someone courageously imagined replacing a damaged heart with a new one. Imagine that! Now we can transplant many organs and can even create artificial ones, giving people new lives. All thanks to those who had the courage to authentically imagine their dreams.

Authentic imagination is generous and benefits the entire

world. Reflect for a moment on the potential inspiration and example you can offer those whose lives you touch by imagining your own dream into reality. Your victory, in a soul sense, become everyone's victory. So in truth your dream becomes a gift to the world.

Keep your imagination garden fertilized with input that feeds your dreams. Read what supports your creativity. Look at images that reflect what you want. Pray and meditate for inspiration. Dare to go further than those before you. Dare to bypass the images that restrict you. Dare to imagine your authentic Heart's Desire.

WEEDING THE GARDEN

If your imagination is your garden, then worry is the weed you have to watch out for. Worry weeds sneak up on you, and if you don't watch out, they can spread like wildfire and take over.

The most common worry weed I run into is the "yeah, but" weed. This is a mental state wherein you imagine all sorts of potential disasters visiting you if you dare to plant your dream. "Yeah, but" weeds are scary and prevent you from imagining what you want.

For example, you may want to plant the mental seed of starting your own business. But before you even begin, you encounter the "yeah, but" weed.

"Yeah, but the competition is fierce!"

"Yeah, but according to *Time* magazine, the changes of succeeding are less than five percent in the first year."

"Yeah, but what if I fail?!"

These "yeah, but" weeds are insidious, resilient, and very frustrating when they pop up full-blown in your mind, but recognize them for what they are—your fears.

Another weed that defiles your creative garden is the "logical" weed. Less overwhelming than the "yeah, but" weed but just as devastating to your garden, it works like this.

Imagine you want to plant the mental seed of good health. But as you begin to till the soil of your imagination, the "logical" weed jumps up:

"They haven't found a cure yet."

"Don't get your hopes up—most people don't make it."

The "logical" weed is made up of other people's opinions, not facts.

Yet a third kind of weed you may encounter as you begin to plant your dream is the "realistic" weed. This is the trickiest weed to spot because it often looks like the flower of reason. It projects your anxieties as set in stone, unshakable realities, and hold your imagination hostage. The "realistic" weed usually shows up shortly after your planted seed sprouts and you are just beginning to get excited in anticipation that your dream is coming true.

This weed may stop you every time you think about your dream.

"You may want to be a dancer, but *realistically*, you're too old."

"You may want to meet your soul mate, but *realistically*, you never meet new people."

"You may want to change your profession, but *realistically*, who's going to hire someone as inexperienced [or as overqualified] as you?"

If your imagination is overgrown with weeds of worry, imagine ripping them out and throwing them into a refuse pile. Then prevent them from returning by diligent daily visualizations.

One creative client shared with us her favorite weed-busting technique. She filled an atomizer with lavender water, and every time she imagined a worry weed, she spritzed the air with lavender water and said, "Die, weed! Die!" She loved the physical act of attacking the worry weeds head-on, and she came to associate the smell of lavender with feeling in charge of what grew in her garden.

The best way to keep your garden free of weeds is to watch, notice, and imagine eliminating them before they grow into problems.

PUT A FENCE AROUND YOUR DREAMS

Protect your imagination garden from the "varmints" and pests of negativity, those people who would steal your dreams away. Protect it from the scavengers and blight of cynicism. Don't share it with those who would damage the sprouts as they work toward the surface with discouraging words. Finally, water your imagination garden with daily doses of love.

Don't use your imagination to envy the garden of another. We all choose the images that mold our lives. If another's garden is compelling, use it as a model and be grateful for the inspiration.

CAN YOU POSSIBLY IMAGINE?

Remember that real imagination is propelled by what you are deeply and *naturally* interested in. It follows what you care about. If you simple cannot imagine your Heart's Desire, perhaps it is not your Heart's Desire after all.

My friend Lydia said her Heart's Desire was to go back to school and finish her abandoned degree, but when she tried this exercise, she couldn't imagine herself actually in school.

"What do you imagine instead, Lydia?" I asked.

Lydia answered, "I imagine not needing a degree to success. I imagine continuing in sales and prospering without having to stop and return to school."

"Well, that is your true Heart's Desire," I said. "You cannot imagine school because it is not compelling to you. But work is. Has anyone asked you for your degree?"

"No... not really. I'm just afraid one day I will be asked, and I'll be embarrassed or lose out because I don't have one."

"It's possible, but there is no degree like proven success. Why don't you create the Heart's Desire of success based on personal experience instead of school?"

Lydia had to agree that going back to school was a "should" goal and not truly interesting. But succeeding—now that *was* interesting!

She began imagining graduating from the "school of practical experience" and indeed began to relax about her unfinished studies. The last I heard, she was the vice president of sales in her company and was beginning to make plans to work for herself.

IMAGINE IN THE FIRST PERSON

Many people become frustrated with Principle Number Three because they cannot imagine their spouse, boss, or some other significant person cooperating with what they truly want. My client Shelly brought this up in one Heart's Desire workshop.

"What happens when you can't imagine someone changing and doing what you want? For example, I want my boyfriend to marry me, and he's a die-hard bachelor who swears he'll never marry. Do I imagine him changing? I can't, knowing who he is and how he feels."

I told Shelly that no one can use their imagination to influence someone else's free will. Instead I suggested she imagine either enjoying the relationship as is—if she could—or getting married to the right person who shared the same life goals. In other words, use her imagination to lead her to her dream and not try to force her boyfriend to subject himself to her will.

I also told Shelly that even if her boyfriend did marry her under coercion, he would still be the same person and would most likely be very resentful and angry at her after the wedding. I've seen this happen—a lot.

The right use of imagination requires that you create without manipulation. It worked for me.

My own husband, Patrick, told me when we were dating that we *not* interested in marriage at all. Disappointed, because I loved him, I had no choice but to accept what he wanted. Yet I still wanted to be married, so I said good-bye to him. Three weeks later he proposed to me in the most romantic fashion at the foot of the Great Pyramid in Cairo.

When I said good-bye to Patrick, I meant it. I knew from my spiritual teachings that I had to honor his wishes, and I followed my Heart's Desire to be in a loving, committed marriage. But when he got what he wanted, he changed his mind. (Don't we all, from time to time?) Once Patrick realized my intentions were set, with or without him, he chose to join me. Twelve years and two children later, he's still a hundred-percent-committed great husband.

In other words, if what you want seems impossible, imagine being surprised with something *better*. When you imagine your dream, don't force anything. If your dream involves cooperation from someone, turn it over to God.

I do this by saying

Divine Spirit, bring to my dream all necessary support.

And then let the Universe work on it.

The imagination is where genius is born. Turn yours back on. Feel your desire with images that excite and motivate.

Every dream involves you! Envision your dream as a movie with you starring in the lead role. How do you feel? Just follow that feeling, and it will lead you to the center of your dream.

Now let's move on to practicing Principle Number Three.

PRACTICING THE THIRD PRINCIPLE

IMAGINING YOUR DREAM

Every night just before you go to sleep, focus your full attention on imagining your dream as if it were happening now. Eliminate everything else from your inner vision. Think only of what you want.

How would your desire affect you if realized? How would you feel? Where would you be? What would you be doing? How would it help you? How would others see you? What would be different? Imagine the answers to these questions. Experience your dream in pictures, words, emotions—whatever your imagination gives you, in whatever way it comes. If your goal is a true Heart's Desire, this exercise will come easily.

Do this same exercise upon awakening first thing in the morning. Every day, imagine new details—sights, sounds, smells, sensations, emotions. Imagine it from all angles. Don't see your dream in a flat, faraway, black-and-white fashion. Give it color, sound, texture, tone, motion, rhythms—life force. Ask yourself, "Can I truly *imagine* being at the center of my Heart's Desire?" Then imagine it, in living color. Imagine how your world would be different with your Heart's Desire in it. Allow this to be a private luxuriating experience.

Don't rush through your imaginings. Enjoy yourself.

IMAGINATION BOOSTERS

- Write your Heart's Desire on colorful pieces of paper.

- Carry your Heart's Desire list everywhere you go, in your wallet or your purse.

- Meditate on the feelings and emotions of your Heart's Desire every morning while you shower.

- Sing your Heart's Desire song on your way to work, driving home, cleaning house, fixing dinner—anywhere you think of it.

- Every day, imagine another detail about your dream that will bring you pleasure.

- Build a fence around your dream. Do not tell anyone what you are creating. Save the energy to *create* instead!

YOUR IMAGINATION GARDEN RITUAL

Take fifteen minutes a day to mentally tend your imagination garden. Just before bed is often a good time. Because the subconscious mind responds very well to ritual, pick a special outfit to wear when going into your creative garden. (Pajamas are fine, if they are special.) Putting on special clothes will prime your subconscious mind and put it into the receptive mode.

Since ancient times, all priests and holy men have worn sacred clothing to illustrate that important, soulful work is going on. (And they often looked like pajamas!) By wearing a special garment when working, you get all the creative circuits in your soul operating and releasing into the ethers the best of your creativity.

One thing I have learned over time is that to really engage my imagination, it helps to do something physical to boost it. I boost my own imagination by engaging all of my senses in this creativity ritual.

First, I put on my sacred kimono (a Japanese wraparound kimono from Chinatown), and I tell my subconscious mind that I am going into my imagination garden. I bring a notebook and pen. Next, I light incense and candles. My favorite incense is copal, because it has a rich, earthy smell and was used in ancient temple blessings. My candles are beeswax, but only because I like beeswax candles!

Then I play special meditation music. I have several favorite CDs that have natural sounds of birds, running water, wind breezes with flute accompaniment. The music sets the ambiance I need to start dreaming.

When I have created the proper ambiance, I close my eyes and meditate on my Heart's Desire. I try to envision it as a movie that I am starring in , rather than simply watching from afar. I enjoy my creative movie for a few moments, then open my eyes. Finally, I write down what I want to create, and then I read it back, out loud.

This entire ritual takes fifteen to twenty minutes, and I enjoy it so much that I look forward to it every day. Try creating your own imagination garden. There is no "proper" way to do this. Trust your natural instincts and allow yourself to invent your ritual with a sense of childlike play. Don't censor your dream or try to downscale it to realistic size. The imagination is where all invention is born, and it needs to be unleashed with sensuality and abandon. By doing this, you will create the necessary passion to set your dream in motion.

PUTTING YOURSELF IN THE PICTURE

Tape your Heart's Desire to a large mirror somewhere in your home. Because of the need to protect your dream, this mirror should not be in public view for others to see. It can be on the back of a closet door or at a writing desk. Use your imagination to hide your mirror.

Tape your Heart's Desire statements on this mirror, along with photos, magazine pictures, cards, or any other visual aids. Place them all around the edges, leaving a circle in the middle for your beautiful face to shine back at you, surrounded by your dreams. Write the words "So Be It," and tape them to the top and bottom of the mirror.

Look into your mirror at least once every day.

MUSICAL IMAGINATION TOUR

Choose a favorite CD or MP3 to listen to when you want to focus on imagining your dream. It doesn't matter what type of music you select, as long as it evokes the emotion you desire. Avoid the blues—unless, of course, you are a masochist and desire pain, loneliness, and rejection!

67

Describe Your Desires as Sensually as You Can		
DESIRE #1	**DESIRE #2**	**DESIRE #3**
Sight		
Sound		
Smell		
Taste		
Touch		

MEDITATION

Before beginning this meditation, you may want to choose some quiet, soothing music for background. It can be whatever is calming to you—nature sounds or classical, New Age, or meditation music. This can be found at any music store.

Find a comfortable, quiet spot where you can lie down, stretch out, and relax. Take a few deep breaths and then exhale, allowing your eyes to close.

Imagine that it is a beautiful day. The sun is warm. The sky is blue. Imagine that you are quietly relaxing and watching the sights all around you.

Now imagine that a messenger approaches you with a notice that something special is waiting for you in your mailbox. Allow excitement, delight, wonder, and anticipation to fill you as you begin walking toward the box. Great expectations rise up in your heart. Who can be sending you something? Let your imagination soar as you take each step.

Eventually, let yourself come to a shiny red mailbox with your name printed in bold letters across the side. Allow yourself to feel your excitement as you open this bright red mailbox and reach inside.

As you pull your hand out of the mailbox, notice that what you have retrieved is a packet of seeds.

On the front of this packet is a very clear picture of your Heart's Desire—the secret wish that you always have in your dreams.

Allow yourself to know that these seeds contain the unique wish that you carry in the deepest core of your being. It is in your dreams. It is in your worries. It is even, at times, in your nightmares. It is what makes up your fantasies.

It is exactly *what you want to do with your life.*

Hold this magical packet of seeds to your heart for a moment, then imagine the perfect place to plant your seeds, the place you can create a sacred garden for your special dream. Allow yourself to go to that place.

Once you are at the spot where you will plant your garden, look around you and find a tool to begin working the soil.

Pick it up and begin tilling the soil of your garden slowly… Take your time and pull up all the weeds. Lovingly clear away the pebbles and stones as you prepare this garden to grow your dreams. As you work, feel how right this place will be for those seeds to be planted.

Now reach down and pick up a handful of soil from your garden. Allow yourself to know intuitively what it needs. It is moist? Is it dry? What does it need from you? More love? More attention? More commitment? More focus? What can you give your plot of ground to nourish your seeds into maturity?

Turn the soil with your own hands until it is loose and friable. Take the time to smell its rich scent. Lift up a handful and inhale. Smell the anticipation of the soil.

Now, very carefully, open your seed packet and take out these seeds, allowing them to represent to both your conscious and unconscious mind the full potential of your Heart's Desire.

Carefully, lovingly, and with great focus of intention,

sprinkle these seeds into the ground. Use your hands to cover the seeds with earth.

Then take the seed packet, place it on a stick, and place it in the middle of your garden, so that the picture of your Heart's Desire is visible each time you visit the garden.

Now, with your intention, make a protective fence and put it all around your garden. Then stand back to admire your work.

Imagine yourself nourishing this garden with love and devotion. See yourself checking it every day. Be patient until the seeds germinate. Do not uproot the seeds with impatience. Have faith that they will grow. Be aware of the crows and rabbits that will want to steal your special dreams.

See yourself standing up as a mighty force to anything that might try to rob you of your Heart's Desire. Banish from your garden anything that does not encourage growth.

Know that sometimes the rain will wash your seeds, sometimes it will be your sweat, and sometimes it will be your tears. Know each day that nothing can stop these seeds from growing. Above all, know that you have planted your dreams with love.

You may see what others have planted. You may see their ideas and dreams harvested in the garden right next to yours. Use their efforts as encouragement, but never lose faith that your dreams are sprouting beneath the surface. Your own dreams are unfolding and reaching for life.

Now take a breath and focus on the energy that flows through you. Let it flow through you and through your garden, and see your dreams beginning to awaken.

See the new sprouts bursting to life as your dreams climb above the surface. See them reaching for life… beginning to grow… reaching higher and higher… growing stronger and more powerful each day.

Remember that you do not make these seeds grow. They

*grow in spite of your worrying. They have their own energy
and power as they are supported and fed by the earth and
energized by the sun.*

*The garden grows because it desires fulfillment and
fruition of the seeds you have planted.*

*Stand back again and admire your work. Watch your
dreams grow stronger and more powerful, with deep roots and
high branches. See the blossoms flowering and bearing the fruit
of your dreams.*

*Now, celebrate the harvest. Take a few moments to breathe
quietly so you can enjoy the manifestation of your dream.*

When you are ready, slowly open your eyes.

REVIEW

If you can successful and sensually imagine your dream, move on
to Principle Number Four.

If you can't, go back and review Principles One, Two, and Three
to see what might be missing.

PRINCIPLE NUMBER FOUR

Eliminate Your Obstacles

The first three Principles are like the architect of your dream, carefully designing the blueprint of your Heart's Desire. Once the energy needed to create your dream is sufficiently gathered, you are ready to begin moving your dream into expression. Principle Number Four engages the Creative Contractor, the aspect of Divine spirit that begins to *builds* your dream on earth.

I first learned about Principle Number Four when I was fourteen years old. It was a time in my life when my greatest Heart's Desire was to develop my intuitive ability to the highest degree possible. I pored over volumes and volumes of metaphysical books. I studied tarot decks and did readings with ordinary playing cards by the hour. I wore bandannas, hoop earrings, bracelets up to each elbow, and swirling skirts and pretended I was "Madame Sonia, Psychic Extraordinaire." But what I really wanted was to apprentice with a master.

One day my mother told us that she had invited a very special person to dinner. His name was Charlie Goodman, a renowned spiritual teacher who possessed the most extraordinary gifts of clairvoyance, clairaudience, and trance channeling. He had a following all over the world, and we were very fortunate that he would be joining us.

I was so excited that I changed clothes three times just so I would look my best. When Charlie was introduced to me, my heart was pounding so hard, it nearly pushed through my chest. Charlie was a sweet man about seventy years old with white hair and thick glasses. He chain-smoked Marlboro cigarettes and had a contagious laugh that sounded to me like a babbling brook.

During dinner Charlie sat at the head of the table and, one by one, gave each member of our family a short reading and told us the names of our master teachers and spirit guides.

When he came to me, he said, "Sonia, your spirit guide is Michael the archangel. You have the gift of intuitive knowing, and you will help people find peace in their lives..."

My head swooned. He noticed that I was intuitive—I was so flattered!

He continued, "...if you learn to develop it."

Rats! I thought I *was* learning.

After dinner I mustered the courage to ask Charlie to teach me to speak with guides, and he agreed. "If you can be disciplined enough, Sonia, I will help you."

We arranged to meet at noon on Saturday a week later. On the first Saturday we were to meet, I arrived at Charlie's house at twelve-fifteen and rang the bell. There was no answer.

I was confused, then worried, but I waited awhile. Finally, after Charlie failed to appear, I left and looked for a phone. I called Charlie's number, but the phone just rang and rang. Charlie was definitely not there.

Disappointed and slightly annoyed, I went home. "Maybe he's senile and forgot," I thought to myself. I called several times during the week, but there was still no answer.

The next Saturday came, and I called Charlie before I left to make sure he'd be there. To my surprise, this time he answered.

"Hello, Charlie here!" he said.

"Charlie, this is Sonia. What happened last week? We were

supposed to meet at noon."

"That's right," he said. "Where were you? I waited until twelve-ten, then I left. You were not here at noon as we had agreed."

"But Charlie, I can't believe you left! I caught a late bus, and had to do a few things, and I was just a *little* late."

"Too late to be serious, Sonia!" he said. "You were avoiding being on time."

I tried to explain my tardiness, but he cut me off. Charlie wasn't interested in why I was late. He said our classes were an appointment with spirit, which needed to be honored with promptness.

"Spirit guides do not care about excuses. If they gather enough energy to come through to our plane of consciousness, and you are not there, then you are not serious. If it's important, *really* important, you will put your life in order and make it your priority. This means being on time. Spirit is organized, and if you want to work with spirit you must be organized, too. Don't ever waste your time on distractions when working on a goal. Time is all you have of any importance."

Perhaps he was right, I thought. Perhaps I was much too casual about such an important Heart's Desire by giving it the top priority in my life. He taught me that to realize your Heart's Desire, you have to commit to doing everything in your power to make it happen—first thing, not last. I learned not to make excuses about avoiding the work. With Charlie I learned to evaluate my behavior with insight and honesty, and I realized that to protect my dream I had to drive away the distractions and be fully available to what I desired.

My classes with Charlie took place twice a week, and to continue with him I had to eliminate whatever stood in the way.

"Charlie," I'd test him occasionally, "can't you be flexible?"

"I can," he'd say, laughing, "but Universal law won't be. If you truly want something, Sonia, you must be unyielding in your desire to protect it and unwavering in your commitment to it. That means not being lazy or flaky about it!"

In my studies with Charlie I learned the skills of clairvoyance (the art of seeing future events), clairaudience (the art of listening to spirit guides), psychometry (the art of "reading" objects), and trance channeling (the art of allowing a spirit guide to speak through you)—all miraculous tools in my life. But in retrospect, I believe the greatest tool I developed was the unwavering decision to commit my full energy to my Heart's Desire. I learned *to organize my life around my dream, rather than try to force my dream into my chaotic life.* By doing so, I began to lay the foundation of my purpose.

TIME OUT!

Principle Number Four is about time. No matter what you desire, be it spiritual growth or a face-lift, at some point it is going to require some time from you to make it happen. And the only way you are going to find that time is to decide your dream is important—that it is valuable.

In our society, that is difficult. Many students have come to me during my workshops and privately revealed that taking time for themselves feels selfish. The only way they can justify doing this without suffering from guilt is to take care of everyone and everything around them before they attend to their own needs. The problem is that by the time they finish attending to everyone else's emergencies, they have no time (and certainly no energy) to create their own dreams.

I used to think that this was mostly a woman's problem, but after teaching these Principles for ten years, I now believe that men suffer from this dilemma just as often. I think of it as the "you must finish all your homework before you can go out and play" syndrome. It is the internalized parental voice so many of us were raised with.

The trouble is that our work is never done, so playtime, time to focus on what we love, never arrives—or if it does, it is accompanied by a huge dose of guilt that robs us of any real pleasure in our pursuits. This thinking somehow conditions us to believe that it is morally superior to suffer, to put others before ourselves, to work excessively, and to deny ourselves pleasure.

I suspect much of this thinking developed out of confusion over the teachings of one of the greatest spiritual masters, Jesus Christ. Jesus said, "Love your neighbor *as* yourself," but we were taught to hear it as "*instead* of yourself."

Following this mistaken interpretation, we've become a society of tired workaholics, resentfully awaiting our turn in the next life, never quite feeling appreciated for all our sacrifices in this one. And our Heart's Desires are left lurking in the corners of our inner selves, ignored.

The first step in applying Principle Number Four to correct this misconception. Start by realizing that it is your Divine Right to love yourself, and it is Divine wisdom to pursue what your soul requires. This means putting *value* on your needs and committing your time to fulfilling them.

Another obstacle that prevents us from embracing and committing to our Heart's Desires is that we were raised to be approval-seeking creatures, defining our worth through the eyes of those looking at us. We've become enslaved to notions of what was acceptable to others.

ELIMINATE SABOTAGE

One of the first actions to take in support of your Heart's Desire is to protect your dreams with strong boundaries. At this stage they are delicate sprouts barely entering the Universe and need to be surrounded with protection and vigilance. You need to protect your dreams by removing yourself from all nonsupportive influence, such as crucial, jealous, or negative friends, abusive associations, and cynics who have hardened their hearts.

For example, if it is your desire to create health, then remove yourself from all toxic substances, circumstances, and people that throw your psyche and body out of balance. If your desire is prosperity, then remove yourself from poverty-minded people and circumstances in your path.

Mind you, I said remove *yourself*–not to reform everyone around you. I have witnessed hundreds of dreams dashed by a naysayer or a jealous, negative, cynical person telling others that they were crazy or stupid to believe they could have what they wanted. Client after client has said, "My wife thinks I'm crazy," "My husband laughs at me," "My children say I'm out of touch with reality," or "My family won't hear of it."

People mistakenly believe that their dreams need the approval of the people they love in order to manifest. This isn't true. The truth is, you may not find believing and supportive people where you would like to, but the good news it you don't need anyone's approval to succeed. What you *do* need is to protect yourself from demoralizing, dream-damaging, disapproving saboteurs.

Forget wasting time trying to change or convince anybody of the worthiness of your intentions. It will simply siphon away the energy that you need to focus on your dream. Your desire should be treated like a treasure and secreted away from disbelieving eyes. A friend once said, "If someone works against you, deny them you."

Retreat.

Back off.

Go underground.

Be intelligent.

Establish clear and protective boundaries so your dreams will have a chance to become firmly rooted in your life.

DESIRE EQUALS DISCIPLINE

Paul's Heart's Desire was to become a partner in his real estate firm and to enjoy financial success and respect. He was so preoccupied with *appearing* worthy of partnership in his employer's eyes that he shopped for the most expensive clothes, drove a brand-new Lexus, frequented all the pricey, trendy restaurants, and was constantly trying to impress people with how successful he was. The truth was that he didn't have the discipline to earn his success. Instead he thought that looking successful (even while going into debt) was the same as *being* successful. He believed that if he had the approval of others, it would somehow get him what he wanted. He squandered his time and money on appearances instead of simply focusing on his work.

The consequences of Paul's lack of discipline soon became apparent to those around him. He was spending more money than he made and incurring huge debts. Creditors hounded him at work, embarrassing him. He became distracted from focusing on his job and was eventually fired for his lack of productivity. His lack of discipline to work and earn before spending had put him even further behind in his career goals.

Paul never learned what most people come to realize through hard experience—there's no such thing as a free lunch.

Principle Number Four requires you to identify and eliminate everything that takes you away from focusing on your Heart's Desire. *Everything!* It means looking at every plane of energy and noticing any waste, clutter, distraction, or disorder that keeps you from focusing your full attention and energy on your dream. And it means finding the time and discipline to establish the order your dreams require for growth.

Start with the most obvious: your physical surroundings. Chaos, sloppiness, unfinished business, and clutter are energy bandits, stealing away your time! Every moment of time you have to spend looking for things, apologizing, or mentally hiding out from old unfinished business is time you've lost forever.

Is your house in order? Is it stuffed with unnecessary junk? Are you hanging on to something simply (as the explorer said of Mount Everest) "because it's there"?

Clear the decks. Donate. Recycle. Share. Have a yard sale. Make room for new energy and life force to flow into your life.

Joan and Mark, friends of ours, were some of the worst pack rats we knew. They were also two of the most unfulfilled, unhappily employed, and financially strapped people we knew. Buried in junk, they justified their attachments because they worried that they might one day need these artifacts of their past and wouldn't be able to afford them. Their greatest heartbreak was that they couldn't conceive a much-longed-for child, even though they were afraid they couldn't afford to raise one. And the cost of infertility treatments was out of the question.

After coming to a Heart's Desire workshop, they realized that they were spinning their wheels on jobs they didn't like and were straining their marriage over their infertility troubles. After using creative Principles One, Two, and Three, they decided that their Heart's Desire was a fresh start in another city. Embracing Principle Number Four wholeheartedly, they sold their house and gave away or sold their belongings. With their newfound freedom they decided to travel across the country in a leisurely search for a new home base, a luxury that was new to their way of thinking.

They got as far as Colorado, where, while camping on a mountain, they conceived the child they had always wanted. Overjoyed, Joan and Mark realized that emptying their lives of old fearful attachments had opened their hearts and souls to receive what they truly longed for—a family *and* freedom.

As I've grown, I have come to love the Fourth Principle of Creativity more than any other. It is as if I have a "Creativity Sergeant" walking through my life. The Fourth Principle is the Principle of commitment, the champion of order and protection. Its soldiers are elimination and organization. The Fourth Principle moves in like a marching army to establish boundaries, making it possible for your dream (in this most fragile stage) to grow without danger.

Principle Number Four opens the way to progress by asking you to examine your attachments. Are they worth holding on to if they prevent you from reaching for your dream?

TO THINE OWN DREAM BE TRUE

I had a wonderful friend in college whose Heart's Desire was to be a rock musician. Andy had a fabulous voice and played guitar, but he had a huge obstacle course to run. The budding rock musician's world revolved around nightclubs and bars, and Andy came from a strict conservative Christian background, where his family viewed rock music and its attendant milieu of alcohol and clubs as sinful.

Rebellious, Andy attempted to follow his dream for a while, but eventually the estrangement and guilt he felt were too much for him. He gave up his band and decided to be a good son. He found work more acceptable (to his parents) in their church-run hospital.

Though he tried hard to be satisfied with his life, Andy's abandoned love weighed heavily on his heart. He became slowly and subtly depressed. In an attempt to maintain some remnant of his true love, he frequented bars and nightclubs after work and began drinking quite a bit. His depression also manifested itself in insomnia, and through his connections at the hospital he was prescribed tranquilizers. In no time he became addicted to both alcohol and prescription drugs.

We had several conversations over the years, and on many occasions he acknowledged the need to eliminate drugs and alcohol, to eliminate his need for family approval, and to eliminate his attachment to a depressing job. Most of all, he needed to eliminate denying his misery so that he could pursue music, his real love.

But Andy never eliminated his obstacles. Instead his obstacles eliminated him. At the age of thirty-seven he died from an overdose of Valium and wine.

Andy's story is a tragic one, but sadly all too common. So often we wait passively for some outside force to give us permission to be who we are and to champion our cause. My teacher Charlie taught me as a teenager that the permission can come only from within, from our own souls. One day after I had apprenticed with Charlie for years, he asked me to do an intuitive reading for him. Feeling that I was not yet entitled to think of myself as a psychic, I said, "Charlie, I can't."

"Why not?" he said. "What are you waiting for?"

Upon reflection, I finally realized what it was. "Permission," I answered.

Charlie let out a huge belly laugh. "From who?" he asked.

I thought. "From you...?" I half answered, half asked.

Again he laughed. "Sonia, get *rid* of the idea that anyone can give you permission to be who you are! I can't give you permission. No one can. The permission comes from you!"

With Charlie's help I was able to eliminate the idea that I needed someone else to tell who I was. I did my first intuitive reading for Charlie then and there, and I've been doing them ever since—thirty years' worth.

It's important to realize what Charlie helped me to see—that you cannot actually be *whatever* you want. You can only be who you really are, and only you can give yourself permission to express it. Principle Number Four is the equivalent of a metaphysical Roto-Rooter, flushing up and out everything that clogs the pathway to your Heart's Desire. And it is at this point that you need to see your obstacles for what they are and remove them from your path.

Whether it is the physical pollution of disorder, the emotional pollution of drama and martyrdom, the mental pollution of other people's ideas of who you are or should be, the psychic pollution of addiction, or the spiritual pollution of fear and lethargy—now is the time to confront and let go. Now is the time to reevaluate your *time.*

One of the most common mistakes I observe people making when pursuing their Heart's Desires is mismanaging their time and forgetting to plan time for miracle making. I see people spending too much time on things they can delegate or forget altogether. They spend too much time on things they can delegate or forget altogether. They spend their time in fragmented ways, doing a little toward their dream, but not enough to get it going. They fritter away their time on huge energy drains like watching television or talking on the phone or listening to someone else complain.

Not that I don't enjoy TV, or the phone, or that I don't have a sympathetic ear. It's just that there is a time for everything, and Principle Number Four asks you to own your time and use it to support your dream.

Ask yourself frequently during the day, "Is this the best possible use of my time? Or can I let this go?" Even more important, ask yourself, "When am I going to spend some time on my Heart's Desire today?"

Principle Number Four may seem harsh, but don't be deceived. You aren't required to eliminate anything important. You are required to eliminate only what sabotages your progress and smothers your dreams. Though this may seem temporarily stringent, it is actually very freeing and empowering and will reveal whether or not you are serious.

If you are, this Principle will catapult you forward. If you aren't, it will reveal your insincerity and help you stop—a big relief if you are on the wrong track. Either way you are helped by this

Principle. You will eliminate distractions and waste and will also eliminate your goal if it isn't right for you.

Several years ago a woman named Jeannie came to our Heart's Desire workshop. She had a very heavy heart as she told her story.

Jeannie was a hairdresser who learned her profession straight out of high school. She was one of those "nice" people who say yes to everyone. She gave haircuts ten hours a day, worked overtime and weekends, and accommodated everyone's needs, all for a very low salary. Yet as nice as she was, she had few friends and very low self-esteem.

I asked Jeannie what her true Heart's Desire was.

Jeannie said there were three things she wanted more than anything. The first thing was new furniture. She had left home ten years before with her parents' hand-me-downs, and now they were simply junk. The second thing she wanted was to move. She had lived in the same run-down apartment since leaving home and hated returning to it each evening. The third thing Jeannie wanted was new friends and excitement. She was resentful and bored with giving to other people all day long and never receiving any invitations to go out and have fun.

By the time Jeannie finished telling us her true Heart's Desire, she was crying. "I am afraid to move, and I don't have enough money to pay for movers, let alone new furniture. And with no friends to help me..." she trailed off.

"Jeannie," I said, "it's clear that your desire for change and support is sincere and heartfelt, which brings you to the Fourth Principle of Creativity. What you need to do is ask your Creativity Sergeant to come into the situation and help you eliminate those things that are blocking you. What it will take from you is the willingness to let go of your obstacles. Are you willing?"

Jeannie reflected. "Well I do spend a lot of time feeling sorry for myself. Maybe I'll let go of that."

"Sounds like a good start, Jeannie. Try it and see what happens."

"The self-pity is boring me to death," she said. "So even if nothing else happens, I'll at least feel better, right?"

Jeannie left the class with a new resolve. Although she had no way of figuring out how her dreams would come true, she was honestly ready for change and tired of her own sad story.

I forgot about Jeannie until one day, eight months later, I received a letter from her.

"You'll never believe what happened," she wrote. "After I left the Heart's Desire workshop I continued to visualize my dream. I also worked at letting go of my negative emotions and committed myself to change. I was ready.

"Then one day I came home from work to discover firemen swarming all over the block. My apartment building had burned to the ground! Everything I owned was reduced to ashes. Here's where the miracle comes in. When my clients at work heard about what happened, they showed up by the dozens. People I thought only cared about a haircut offered me so much love, support, and furniture, I couldn't believe it. One man even offered me a place to stay and confessed later that he had been attracted to me all along, but didn't know how to say so!

"As for my ratty old furniture, happily it was burned to the ground, too. On top of that, my mother is an insurance agent. She had insured the furniture years ago and kept it in force. I just received a check to replace it all. I'm going shopping today. This has been the most exciting thing that has ever happened to me."

Jeannie's Heart's Desire had come to pass.

In Jeannie's case the Creativity Sergeant of Principle Number Four literally blazed through her life, creating the opening for her dreams to appear. Jeannie's miracle was sudden and unexpected, and it worked out because she was so honestly ready for change. Her experience taught her an important truth—you must let go of what's in your hand to reach for something greater.

Not everyone who has a dream is as honestly willing to let go of their obstacles as Jeannie was. Let me tell you a story about a woman who also had dreams but was not willing to clear the way.

Laura came to me for a reading after she too had taken the Heart's Desire workshop. When she arrived for the reading, she was agitated and wanted to talk more than listen.

"I'm having a very hard time with these creative Principles," she said. "They may sound good, but it's a lot harder than you say to let go of things."

"Laura, I never said letting go of obstacles was easy. I only said it was *necessary* if you want to create your dream. What is it that you are unable to let go of?"

Laura started crying. "Four years ago I divorced my husband and almost immediately met the perfect guy, John. We were together night and day for two years. Suddenly, without warning, he broke off our relationship when I asked for a commitment. My Heart's Desire is to marry John, yet you suggest I get rid of him! I can't do that. I want just the opposite. I want him back!"

Laura had a problem. Her goal was to marry someone who clearly wasn't interested in committing to her. My reading showed that in their relationship she was controlling and clingy. In dating John, Laura had merely transferred her dependence from her ex-husband. Laura was not committed to her own life and was using John to carry her. Any relationship needs the energy of two balanced partners in order to really thrive. Because Laura was leaning so heavily on John for her identity, she became a burden and he left.

"Laura," I suggested, "perhaps what you should let go of is the need to be so heavily identified with a man. Perhaps the kind of marriage you want first requires that you find yourself and become committed to you! In other words, create a meaningful life of your own and see what happens."

Laura was upset by my suggestion. Her entire notion of happiness was focused on controlling John. Letting go of that need to control would be a huge shift for her.

"If you want marriage, focus on marriage. But the kind of marriage you desire is based on love and friendship, not fear and dependency. You've already experienced a dependency-based marriage and you were miserable, remember?"

Laura argued with me. "You're right, I *am* afraid of being alone, but I can't let go of John. And I won't. I know he is right for me, and we're right for each other. I can't believe he won't eventually see it, too."

She left, angry.

Laura missed the point entirely. Principle Number Four requires that you honestly let go of whatever is blocking the way to your dream. In Laura's case, that meant she had to let go of manipulation, fear of independence, and the need to control. I never told her to let go of John. Besides, he was not there for her to let go of.

Laura refused to see how attached she was to attitudes and behaviors that prohibited an honest love from flowing. She continued to pursue John, succeeding only in further alienating him. The following year John suddenly married an attorney.

Laura was devastated, but finally she understood. She went into therapy and enrolled in medical school. Three years later she graduated with honors and was finally able to be independent and proud of herself. She started a private medical practice and soon met another doctor who, like her, had completely reinvented his life. After dating a short while, they eloped and are now living happily in Kansas City.

Laura wrote me a note.

"When we spoke that day, I knew what you said was right, but I wasn't willing to listen. After a lot of heartache, I finally let go of everything. I was trying to control and got on with my life. Surprisingly, I met Leo. He is the best partner, both in work and love. When I finally let go of the wrong thing, I received everything I had dreamt of, and more. Now I understand what Principle Number Four means."

I CAN SEE CLEARLY NOW

The Creativity Sergeant can be difficult if you have a blind spot. Sometimes it shows up spontaneously in answer to your deepest soul desires, even if your conscious mind blocks you. When it does, look out! It is like a lightning bolt, carving a path with fury.

Alicia was a workaholic who devoted twelve to fourteen hours a day to her job as an investment banker at a major international bank. Alicia was driven by an almost manic need to succeed and was desperately out of balance. She came to see me because her Heart's Desire was to have a baby and she had been completely unsuccessful in doing so. At age forty-one, exhausted after three miscarriages, she was desperate.

Dressed in an immaculate business suit and "on a tight schedule," carrying her portable phone and wearing a beeper, she came into the reading saying, "I only have three quick questions. Will in vitro work? How many times will it take? And how much money will it cost?"

Alicia was so addicted to her banking job and all of its wheeling and dealing that she had lost all touch with her feminine side. To her, conceiving a child was another business deal, and she was trying to reduce the risk. In reality, Alicia could go through in vitro fertilization as many times as she wanted, but without a place in her to receive a child, there would be no baby. She was so booked, so busy, and so rushed that couldn't receive another phone call, let alone take on the care and commitment of a newborn.

The first thing I suggested was that she turn off the phone and the beeper and turn her attention inward.

"See what a crowded house it is in there?" I asked. "Where are you going to fit in a baby? There's no room physically or emotionally."

Alicia was not interested in self-reflection. To her, conception all boiled down to doctors, time, and money. She had lost all connection to the soulful process of becoming pregnant. Pregnancy was simply a mechanical process to her. Needless to say, I didn't see a successful in vitro fertilization.

Alicia rushed out, disappointed. She did have in vitro fertilization four more times but did not succeed in conceiving.

Then one day as Alicia was rushing home from work, her car was hit by a taxi running a stop sign. She suffered a broken wrist and ribs and was forced to take ten weeks off from her all-consuming job to recuperate. As with any addict, her first days off work were the worst, but after a few weeks she started to relax and get back in touch with the world around her. She began to meditate and took up yoga. Her recovery turned out to offer a long-overdue hiatus from the intensity of her all-consuming job.

Just before returning to work, Alicia had a final physical exam. Overall she felt recuperated. The only problem was that she was feeling unusually tired, so her doctor ordered a blood test to see if she was fighting an infection or a virus.

The doctor met her in his office and said, "You are on your way, Alicia. Your tests are fine. And you'll never believe this, but your blood-work indicates that you are pregnant! That's why you are feeling tired."

Alicia was stunned. After four years of trying to conceive with no luck, she conceived naturally while recuperating from her accident. She quit her job, started working freelance out of her home, and is now the mother of a beautiful baby boy.

"That taxi plowed into my life in answer to my prayer. I was on automatic pilot and couldn't stop myself. I had to laugh about my miracle. You know how taxis are always rushing. That's what hit me—my own rushing about!"

Principle Number Four came plowing into Alicia's path, removing the greatest obstacle of all to her dream—herself.

ASK YOUR CREATIVITY SERGEANT TO SET THINGS IN ORDER

The Creativity Sergeant may visit you unexpectedly. If it does, it usually first appears as a loss that, upon deeper inspection, reveals itself as a liberation. It may show up in ways that frustrate you, shock you, even sadden you. It may be the force behind the job you lose, the relationship that ends, the illness that stops you in your tracks. It may even be, as in Alicia's case, the cab that hits you.

If your Heart's Desire is true, if you believe in your dream, and if your imagination is filled with right images, you will find yourself facing the loving but stern visage of your Creativity Sergeant. When this occurs, welcome it into your life!

When you are ready to receive your dream, ask your Creativity Sergeant to step in and take over. Take a look at your life and ask yourself how you can help prepare the way.

Look at how you spend your time. Are you giving your dreams and desires priority? Are you making room for them in your life? Is your dream at the top of the list of things to attend to? Even if the attention involves only your five minutes of visualization, are you placing it first in your life or after everything else?

Look at your environment. Is it cluttered with stuff you will never use again? Are you attached to old things out of fear of want or a reluctance to let go of the past? Are you distracted from concentrating on the important work of your true desires by giving unimportant things your attention? Are you rushing so fast that you can't even take a moment to inhale? Are you self-indulgent and undisciplined?

Keep a critical lookout for these energy-sucking monsters—are they pushing you into a corner?

- Phone calls with whiners who waste your time
- Television as a filler
- Clutter as an obstacle course
- Memorabilia turned into emotional cement
- Daily doses of doubt (self-talk about how useless, worthless, impossible, pointless, or unlikely your chances of happiness and fulfillment are)
- Complaining as a sport
- Being wimpy when it comes to saying no or being self-reliant
- Overcommitting to others
- Undercommitting to yourself
- Dragging the baggage of other people's ideas about who you are and what you can achieve or express everywhere you go
- Feeling sorry for yourself
- Being lazy or slothful
- Tolerating saboteurs who work against you

You get the idea. Engage your Creativity Sergeant to stop these problems!

Principle Number Four means you are serious about your dream, that you are willing to be honest and practical about what you must do to make a place for it in your life. Even thinking is an action and can be the most powerful action of all when it comes to creating miracles. Principle Number Four is decision. It is giving yourself permission to experience the miracle of your Heart's Desire.

Give up the flakiness! Give up the excuses. Give up the drama. Give up the mess. Give up attachments to the wrong things and ideas, and use that freed-up energy to cut a wide swath for your dream to enter your experience. Give up surrendering your potential to others. Use discipline as your protector, and honor yourself and your Heart's Desire by creating a golden circle of protection around it and yourself. Refuse to let anything sneak into this golden circle and interfere with your miracle!

Commitment is the name for Principle Number Four. Commitment creates the environment for your dream to break through safely.

Commitment is the Creative Contractor breaking ground for your miracle, so get ready... When you do, things begin to happen!

Now back to you.

PRACTICING THE FOURTH PRINCIPLE

HOW DO YOU SPEND YOUR TIME?

For three days, record how you spend your time. Are your priorities in order? How much time do you take for your Heart's Desire? When do you take this time? Can you think of a better time? Are you giving it *enough* time?

WRITE DOWN YOUR FINDINGS.

....

....

....

....

....

....

....

....

THE ROTO-ROOTER: UNCLOGGING THE FLOW

Examine your life. Ask yourself if there is anything blocking your progress or holding you back. If so, what's the attachment? Can you let it go? What is blocking you from creating your dream...

PHYSICALLY? (This means in your environment. Does anything have to go, like a job, a home, a wrong car, junk, outworn articles... or people who don't support you?)

....

....

EMOTIONALLY? (This means excuses, flakiness, insincerity, manipulation, self-pity, addiction, poor judgment, negativity, cynicism, waste, gossip, lying, envy, dependency, irresponsibility, and laziness.)

....

....

MENTALLY? (This means presumptuousness, approval seeking, arrogance, selfishness, fear, drama, denial, intimidation, and avoidance.)

....

....

SPIRITUALLY? (This means closed-mindedness, guilt, shame, low self-esteem, martyrdom, materialism, and general lack of soulfulness.)

....

....

COMMITMENT PACT

Now list what, when, and how you are going to eliminate your obstacles.

Eliminate	WHAT	WHEN	HOW	HOW YOU FEEL ABOUT IT
PHYSICALLY				
EMOTIONALLY				
MENTALLY				
SPIRITUALLY				

MEDITATION

Close your eyes and center yourself both physically and mentally with a few calming deep breaths.

> *Now bring your full attention to your Heart's Desire. Ask yourself whether there is anything that is blocking you from embracing your dream today. Do you have time to care for your dream? If not, what is taking your time? Can you let it go?*
>
> *Do you have space to care for your dream? If not, what is using up your space? Can you let it go?*
>
> *Do you have energy for your dream? If not, what is consuming your energy? Can you let it go?*
>
> *Is there anything in your life, in your past, or in your attitude that is preventing you from receiving your dream today? If so, imagine a huge dump truck is here to collect everything that you no longer want to block you from your Heart's Desire. Imagine tossing all your blocks into the back of the truck. Then watch the truck drive away.*
>
> *Notice how liberated you feel as you are now fully ready to commit to creating your Heart's Desire. Enjoy this feeling peacefully for a few moments.*
>
> *When you are ready, slowly open your eyes.*

REVIEW

Finally, with the bright spotlight of commitment on your dream, move on to Principle Number Five.

If you can't, go back and review Principles One through Four to see where you got off track.

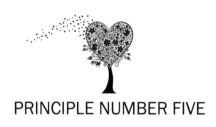

PRINCIPLE NUMBER FIVE

Be Open to Intuitive Guidance

When you come to Principle Number Five, you have reached the halfway point in the creative Principles of manifestation. It is at this point that your conscious efforts will be joined by those of the Universe. Because you are clearing the way to your Heart's Desire, you are now able to expand your consciousness and receive the guidance of your intuition.

Intuition means "inner teacher," and Principle Number Five is about creating a connection with this inner teacher. Intuition is not random, nor it is a fluke. It is the logical next step in the creative process of manifestation, the natural outcome of establishing cooperation among your conscious focus, your subconscious mind, your imagination, and your commitment. It is the predictable consequence of aligning your conscious energy with your intention.

At this stage in the process of manifestation, spiritual guidance begins to play a major part in leading you toward success. As my teacher Dr. Tully taught me, "Once you do your part to reach for your Heart's Desire, the Universe will meet you halfway."

As we begin to control our minds and believe in ourselves, we reawaken to the truth that we are spiritual beings and that, as such, Divine consciousness is constantly seeking ways to express itself through us. By consciously preparing ourselves for this spiritual awakening, we become receptive to spiritual guidance in the form of our sixth sense—our psychic sense—connecting to our Higher Selves. This awakening turns our efforts into a delightful series of synchronicities, psychic insights, spontaneous "Ah-hah!" moments, and inspired solutions. I like to think of this Principle as the moment when the cavalry arrives to help us out!

YOUR GUIDES

The knowledge that spiritual guidance can be received at any time is a revelation to many people. What came as a revelation to me, as a student of Charlie Goodman, my spiritual mentor, was just *how much* support and guidance are readily available. Charlie told me that each of us has a set of guides—spiritual guardians whose sole function is to guide us to our dreams.

What amazed me was the idea that we each have thirty-three guides, mobilized into specific areas of support, working with us at any given time. Imagine that! You have an entire spiritual staff at your service once you become receptive to accessing this guidance.

The Universe, in its loving generosity, has provided guides for everything! And each of us has different guides for different assignments. They are as follows:

Runners	Guides to help you locate things that you have lost or need to find
Helpers	Guides to offer inspiration or solutions as you work on specific tasks
Healers	Guides who direct you in achieving wellness and balance
Teachers	Guides who lead you to information and learning

Joy guides	Guides who amuse you and offer you comic relief
Angels	Beings of light who protect you and keep you from harm
Master teachers	Guides who direct your heart, such as Jesus, Moses, Buddha, Mohammed, White Eagle, Mother Mary, Yogananda, Sai Baba, Mother Meera... The list goes on and on.

PREPARING FOR GUIDANCE WITH MEDITATION

The most important way to prepare for guidance is to meditate. Meditation is an essential part of becoming receptive to Divine spirit. Even if you can meditate for only five minutes a day, the return for your efforts will be exponential.

All of us need to take the time to expand our mental awareness in order to hear inner guidance. Meditation is a relief from the stormy seas of our own thoughts. It calms those seas and soothes away our anxieties. And it doesn't have to be complicated. The slow act of breathing in and saying, "I am," then breathing out and saying "Calm" ten times is an easy start.

All the great spiritual masters, from the teachers of India, China, and Japan to the saints, priests, and mystics of Western cultures, have sought to teach the importance of meditation. Now even Western doctors, healers, and business leaders are beginning to agree that meditation is a key to expanding awareness and heightening creativity. Jesus said it best: "Ask and it will be given. Seek and you will find. Knock and the door will be opened to you."

So, the first step to receiving guidance is to begin meditation every day. This essential commitment to quieting the mind's chatter and turning your focus inward toward your heart, the seat of your soul, is the beginning of a whole new way of living.

The decision to meditate reflects the way the Principle work.

You can't listen on the telephone if someone else is talking to you at the same time, and you can't listen to inner guidance if your mind is chattering on and on.

Meditation, when practiced regularly, stills this chatter and adjusts your awareness to a higher octave of perception. This higher level of consciousness is tranquil and calm, and beyond it is the still, small voice of your Higher Self.

MEDITATIVE ASKING

Once you have learned to quiet your mind's chatter with meditation, you can use meditation to directly ask for guidance. To many people this is such a revelation that they can hardly believe it's so simple—but it is. If you ask, you will receive. That's Universal law.

As a child I watched my mother go into a meditative state to ask for guidance on many occasions. I remember one event in particular because she was so excited about the way her guidance came to her.

Many years ago my mother took up the hobby of oil painting on black-and-white photos, a specialized technique that was very popular at the time. She loved the contemplation and creativity each work afforded her and eventually became so good at this that she began to enter national photography contests in the oil painting division.

One year the National Association of Professional Photographers sponsored a contest that my mother entered. They sent everyone a black-and-white photo of a beautiful young woman in a broad-brimmed summer hat. My mother set to work on this portrait and worked diligently, day and night, for over three months. She completed her work to near perfection but was having a terrible problem getting the paint to set and dry, making it impossible to ship the portrait to the sponsor for judging.

Many days and nights passed without the paint setting

properly, and the contest deadline was fast approaching. My mother remained intently focused on coming up with a solution, in spite of the fact that she was beginning to panic.

One night she threw her arms up in the air in frustration and said, "That's it! I'm going to sit in this chair quietly and not move until the answer comes." And she sat down.

We kids knew better than to disturb her. She was in one of those "don't you even dare make a peep" moods that we never tested.

And she sat. Eyes closed. And sat. Eyes open, staring into space. And sat. Eyes closed...open...staring...closed. For hours. My dad shooed us off to bed. Even he didn't dare interrupt. My mother was waiting for guidance. Eventually, I assume, she fell asleep.

I woke up much later that night, hearing excited voices coming from my parents' bedroom.

"Paul! Wake up. Paul!" My mom's voice floated across the hallway.

"What is it?" he asked drowsily. I listened from my room as he lurched up in bed.

"I fell asleep in the chair, and dreamed I was talking to the painter Raphael. He was standing with me, looking at the painting. He told me that cobalt drier was what it needed! Get up and get me some. I'm sure it will work!" she said excitedly.

"Now?" my father said plaintively. "It's four A.M. Go to bed! I'll get it tomorrow."

And he did, first thing in the morning.

My mother applied the cobalt drier, a rather obscure paint-setting agent, just as Raphael had advised. As promised, the paint set beautifully. Two days later the painting was shipped to the convention for judging. My mother won first place.

The answer had come when stopped taking, thinking, agonizing. It came to her when she quieted her mind and asked for guidance from one of her helpers. She then created the mental quiet to listen for the answer.

BE FLEXIBLE

Frequently you may be made aware of guidance and then struggle to suppress or ignore it. Guidance may urge you to be spontaneous, to try something new, or to deviate from your beaten path and your ingrained habits. When you do respond to your spiritual guidance, however, you frequently stumble upon a whole new way of life that will leave you amazed at the intricate wisdom and workings of Divine law.

Here is a story of two people who recognized and spontaneously responded to spiritual guidance, leading them both to a greater sense of self.

My friend Ruth was married in the 1950s to a character actor. Recently he died, and when I was in New York I asked my friend how their thirty-year-old son, Matt, had taken his father's death.

"He's sad," she said. "It's been very hard for him. But he told me a wonderful story about an angel he met on his flight home."

Ruth said that Matt was very tired and stressed from the vigil at his father's bedside and the myriad demands made on him by the press after the death. His exhaustion was compounded by the commotion at JFK airport. It was five P.M. and the flight was packed.

When Matt entered the cabin, an inner voice compelled him to ask the flight attendant whether he could sit in the relative calm of first class. This was totally out of character for Matt, but he was following his intuition.

"My father just died, and I'm very stressed out," he said to the male flight attendant. "Can I sit up here?"

The flight attendant looked at him and realized that Matt was deep in sorrow and needed help. He paused for a moment, then said, "Sure, I'll work it out." The flight attendant succeeded, and Matt sat in first class.

Once the flight took off and the attendant was serving drinks,

Matt said to him, "Perhaps you know of my father. He was an actor." And he pulled his father's photo out of his wallet.

On seeing the photo, the flight attendant got a very strange look on his face. He said, "Let me finish the service, and then I have something interesting to tell you about your father."

When he finished serving he came back to Matt. "You're going to think this is strange, but I *knew* you were coming. All afternoon I kept seeing your father's face in my mind. I even mentioned it to the other flight attendants because the image was so overwhelming. Now that I've met you, I'm sure your father's spirit was asking me to prepare the way for you."

Matt looked at the flight attendant in astonishment. "Well, that would be just like him." Matt said, "wanting me to go first class. Thank you for telling me."

When Ruth told me this story I was touched. I said, "Doesn't it go to show you how much love and help is available to us all if we only listen to our intuition? What a great story."

But as I found out later, that was only part A. Now let me tell you part B.

The following week Patrick and the girls and I decided to go to my brother's house in Pennsylvania to spend Thanksgiving with him and his wife and three children. My brother and his wife, both flight attendants, had managed the time off from work and were very excited to have us there.

On Thanksgiving Day, after we'd had a sumptuous dinner and were well into dessert, my brother said, "Let me tell you about a strange experience I had a few weeks ago.

"I was flying between Philadelphia and New York when out of nowhere I began to think about an actor I've seen in old movies over the years. I kept saying to myself, "Why am I thinking about him? Well, on the next leg of my trip, from New York to L.A., a very distressed young man got on the flight and told me his father had just died, and asked me if he could sit in first class. Normally I would have said no, but this guy was a wreck, and I felt compelled to bend the rules."

By now I was all ears. Could it be...?

My brother continued, "After we were in the air, he showed me a picture of his father, and I realized that this was the man whose face I had been seeing. It was as though his father had come to me and asked me to take care of his son.

"Isn't that a strange experience?" my brother concluded with a bemused smile.

Shaking my head, I said, "Do you realize I've already heard this story from that man's mother? She's a friend of mine."

Neither of us could believe it, yet... of course!

This incident was a beautiful example of how Principles of Creativity work like falling dominoes. Matt *desired* an emotional respite (the First Principle), *believed* it to be possible when he noticed the empty first-class seats (the Second Principle), *imagined* himself sitting in one (the Third Principle), and, overcoming his normal reserve (the Fourth Principle), followed his intuition by *asking* to sit there (the Fifth Principle). And the Universe cooperated by preparing my brother in advance for the opportunity to help.

Many people have reported this kind of synchronicity when in a severe crisis or emergency. In fact, bookstore shelves are filled with books on the subject of angels and other Divine interventions—in other words, the Fifth Principle in action.

This interplay demonstrates the graceful choreography of Divine guidance as it moves into our consciousness. It affirms so well our connection to the loving Universe and to one another, assuring us that we are never truly alone.

ASK. DON'T DEMAND

Asking for guidance requires a sincere, open heart. If some people err on the side of not asking, there are others who arrogantly demand what they are not able to receive.

I experienced this several times as I was doing a lecture series across the country for *The Psychic Pathway*. On two occasions people approached me and said something like "I want a teacher like the ones you had. How can I contact them?" When I explained that both of them had passed away from years before and I had no personal knowledge of other master teachers I could recommend, they became indignant.

"Why not? Isn't that your *job?!*" one young man demanded. Another woman got very upset and accused me of not directing her to someone because I was selfish.

When I questioned these people about what steps they had taken to prepare for a teacher, they both looked at me in an odd way. "What do you mean?" they asked.

I answered with the following story.

There was once a young man who had heard of a holy master living on a remote mountain in the Himalayas who could teach enlightenment. Desiring to learn, the young man bought an airplane ticket and eventually made his way to the master's hut. He arrived at the master's door, knocked, and announced that he desired enlightenment.

The master answered the door and, after giving him the once-over, shut the door in the young man's face without saying a word.

Surprised and angry, the young man went away, only to come back two days later. Pounding on the master's door, he said, "I spent money to get here! I am ready to be enlightened!"

The door remained closed.

Three more days passed, and the young man pounded angrily on the door again, shouting, "What kind of master are you? I think you won't answer the door and teach me because you are a phony!"

Once again he was met with an unopened door and silence.

Weeks passed, and every day the young man returned and tried to get the master to receive him. Finally, one day he asked the master to *please* teach him. The master's door remained shut.

Weeks passed into months, and still the young man had no success. One day, as the young man was about to turn away from the closed door, the master stepped out and began to walk down the path. The astonished young man rushed to the master's side, almost falling over his words as he walked along with him.

"Please teach me, master. I'm sorry for my rudeness. I'm very sincere. Just tell me what to so." And on and on. All the while the master was silent.

Eventually they approached a bridge over a babbling brook. The young man kept talking, and suddenly the master grabbed the young man by his shirt collar, pushed him to the shore, and shoved his head underwater.

The young man struggled with all his might, but the master was stronger and kept the young man's head submerged. Finally the man summoned all his energy and shot up from the water like a geyser.

Stunned, he yelled at the master, "What are you doing? Are you crazy?"

The master released the young man and chuckled. "When you want guidance as badly as you wanted to breathe a moment ago, *then* perhaps you will be ready to receive it."

Spiritual guidance is like a beautiful symphony broadcasting from a radio transmitter. The broadcast is for everyone, but to hear it you need a receiver. Meditation, clear focus, and an open heart make you a psychic receiver. Expecting guidance is like adding an antenna to that receiver, amplifying the receptivity. Trusting the broadcast is like listening to the music. And acting on your guidance is like dancing to the music, allowing it to move you.

REAL SOLUTIONS, NOT SUPERFICIAL ONES

True spiritual guidance is quiet and subtle and will direct your awareness to solutions. But in order to receive spiritual guidance, you must be willing to address the real problems of your life, not the superficial distractions.

Often we may not want to do that. It's so much more compelling to go for instant gratification. Unfortunately this never works, as I learned the hard way.

When I was in my early twenties I felt very insecure about myself and didn't like who I was very much. I hadn't been in a relationship for some time and was feeling like the ugly duckling. I knew I had some difficulties with me self-esteem, but I wasn't willing to look at my problems in any deep way. Instead I fell into the trap of looking for superficial solutions to get what I wanted. I shopped for clothes and shoes to feel better, but it didn't help much.

At one point when I was very lonely, I met a hairdresser who worked in a salon on Oak Street, the chicest shopping street in Chicago. That really impressed me. I thought *he* would surely know what was *really* cool! In no time at all I was confiding in him and complaining about not having a boyfriend and wondering what I could do about it.

After eyeing me very carefully, he said he'd like to help. He convinced me that my prince would never come unless I did something about my "frizzy, mousy-colored hair, and girl, those eyebrows! They have got to *go!*" Luckily for me, he was the one to help.

Wanting to believe that this was indeed my only obstacle to love, I rushed down to his salon full of expectation. How easy this would be. In by nine, out by two, loved by midnight!

I had my hair cut off, colored red, and permed. Then I had my eyebrows plucked to a single hairbreadth, all under his persuasive promise of allure. To add to the impact, he didn't let me see myself until my "sex bomb" makeover was complete.

When I was finished with the ordeal, I looked in the mirror and gasped. I looked like a Little Orphan Annie who had just been goosed! And to add insult to injury, I had to pay $300 for this damage. I cried all the way home.

When my roommates saw me they were alarmed. It took enormous self-control for them not to laugh at me. I wanted to hide my head under a paper bag.

It took almost six months to recover from this mistake and look like myself again. And I never got even one date out of the deal. If I were a guy, I wouldn't have asked me out, either!

So much for dealing with my problems in a superficial way. I would have been much better off spending them money on a few therapy sessions or enrolling in a creativity course. Not that I have a problem with beauty salons. It's only that they are for hair problems, *not* heart problem!

We live in a superficial culture that touts instant gratification. If you don't think so, just look at the success of psychic hot lines. They are jammed. But the real hot line you need to connect with is from your head to your heart, where true psychic guidance is found.

BE WILLING TO BE SURPRISED

In my classes and in my counseling sessions I have seen over and over the struggle between intellect and intuition. If people cannot intellectually perceive answers, they rule out the possibility of answers existing. Yet reflect for just a moment on all the past successes and delights of your life: did you really *know* in advance that life would be so good to you?

Let me tell you a story about how Principle Number Five worked for a client of mine named Lester.

* * *

Lester came to my very first Heart's Desire workshop twelve years ago. I was nervous about teaching the class because I had never done it before, but I was eager to share the Principles. When Lester showed up, I knew I was in trouble. Thick glasses, notebooks, calculator, and tape recorder—Lester looked every bit the chemical engineer that he was. He was reserved, analytical, and argumentative and was going to challenge my every point; I could just feel it.

Lester went along with me in the class as worked step by step through Principles One through Four, but I could tell he felt he was humoring me and wasting his time. He didn't say anything as went through each Principle, but his body language let me and the other students know that he didn't think much of what I was saying.

When we got to the Fifth Principle, Lester had a fit. In his very reserved Asian way, he interrupted.

"Excuse me! Excuse me... but I have to stop you here. Fine! Fine! Focus, imagine! Clean your house! But now you say that if I am quiet, I will be led to my dream. I don't think so. You explain to me how!"

He had drawn his conclusions and was staring me down. Lester had decided that unless he knew in advance how he would get his Heart's Desire, it wasn't possible. Period.

"Lester," I began, "my point is that if you do all this preparation work and are authentically serious about realizing your dream, then your own soul will show you how. And very likely in the most surprising way. That is the Principle. Be receptive to being shown how, and be willing to be surprised."

"No! I can't believe it! Impossible!"

"Lester," I said, "what is your Heart's Desire, anyway?"

"Well, first I want a wife. Very unlikely desire because I am a very rigid, boring man and I never even date. I don't want a mail-order bride either, although some people have advised me to consider this. I am a romantic. I want to be in love.

"Second, I am a chemical engineer for a big laboratory. I dislike my job, but it pays pretty well. I would like to work for myself, but as a chemical engineer my entrepreneurial options are very limited.

"Finally, I despise the weather here and I want to move. I have applied for engineering jobs in warm-weather cities for many years. The only responses I've received had been low-paying demotion positions. So your theory may be fun, but logically speaking, I am very much stuck to my life and cannot see how it can possibly change!"

Underneath this cool, logical façade, Lester's despair was evident to me. "Lester," I said, "as a scientist you learned to experiment, correct?"

"Yes, why?"

"Well, I would only ask you to apply the same rules of experimentation to these Principles as you would to chemistry. I am sure a good scientist never draws conclusions in advance, as you have. Try these Principles honestly. Experiment first, and only then draw your conclusions afterward. Fair?"

Lester thought quietly. "Okay. Fair enough. But—"

"No *but!* Open your mind. It is my hypothesis that if you follow Principles Number One through Four—focus, believe, imagine, and prepare—then Principle Number Five will direct you to your dream. If you are open to it. Are you?"

Lester accepted the challenge. He agreed to give the first four Principles his all.

A few months later Lester received an invitation to his twentieth high school reunion. It was being held on a three-day cruise in the Bahamas. After opening the invitation, Lester threw the letter away. But for some reason he felt uncomfortable when he did this. His inner voice, his intuition, told him to get that invitation out of the trash and think about it.

Lester retrieved the letter and set it aside for two weeks, trying to ignore it. He hadn't even liked his high school experience, he thought. Yet his intuition, his soul, said, "Go!" Finally, giving in to this voice, which was very much out of Lester's conservative, logical character, he signed up for the cruise.

While on the cruise he became reacquainted with a high school friend who had been in his chemistry class. He name was Bonnie, and she lived in Florida, where she ran a small pharmacy. One thing led to another, and Lester and Bonnie fell in love. Lester quit his job, moved to Florida, and started helping Bonnie run the pharmacy.

In a word, he was guided to his miracle by Principle Number Five. The guidance did not come like a carefully planned road map. Quite the opposite. It came in one word—"Go!"

Lester sent us a wedding invitation on which he had written, "Miracles come true!" And inside it said only, "Principle #5. Sincerely, Lester."

ASKING THROUGH PRAYER

Second to meditation, prayer is the way to set up a connection to your Higher Self. The way my mother put it to me was, "Prayer is asking for guidance. Meditation is listening to it."

If prayer makes you uncomfortable, it may be that either you have never been shown how to pray or you were given some version of the self-deprecating "shame on me, I'm so bad I don't deserve to live" form of prayer. This version is definitely *not* a good way to ask for help. The way I was taught to pray is very simple, and it may be useful to you. My morning prayer before I open my eyes, before I even move, is

> *Divine Father, Holy Mother, move me.*
> *Take me this day to my highest good.*
> *Make me aware of all that will guide me*
> *toward my Heart's Desire. Amen.*

This prayer is short and sweet—and effective. It puts me in the frame of mind to be helped, and I am.

Another very effective prayer is

HELP!

Then close your eyes and open your heart.

My husband, Patrick, did that just recently, and here's what happened.

We had purchased a ninety-year-old Victorian home (a story I'll tell you more about later) and were inundated with an awesome amount of work trying to restore it to its original beauty. Though we did hire a contractor, in an effort to control costs Patrick did a great deal of the work himself. The job turned out to be more effort than we'd ever imagined. It was as though we pulled a loose thread on an old sweater and the entire thing unraveled.

Patrick's hours on the job got longer and longer. He worked day and night, sometimes coming home well past midnight, only to return at six in the morning. The expense, time, and slow progress discouraged him, and he began to feel trapped by the mountain of work still waiting to be done.

One late night while laying tile in one of the bathrooms and encountering setback after setback, he screamed out in frustration, "Help, God! Give me a break! This work is too much. I desperately need an adventure."

The next morning over coffee he told me of his outburst. "Look at my hands," he said, and indeed I could see how cracked and sore they were from al the labor. "I wish I were on the other side of the world right now!" he exclaimed.

Being worn-out myself, I empathized, but since we were poor as church mice with all the expenses, it didn't seem likely that any adventures were on the horizon. "Hang in there, Patrick," I said halfheartedly. "This will eventually end." I hardly believed myself at the time.

A month later we met a friend for dinner and shared with him the painful details of our experience. Empathetic, he cheered us on and urged us to relax. That's when Patrick said, "The only way I can relax is to get away from this. I could really use an adventure to forget about my troubles."

Our friend, a traveler himself, paused and then said, "Well, I've been thinking about an adventure myself, perhaps Argentina or Chile. Why don't you come with me?"

I could see anguish sweep over Patrick's face as he considered and then rejected the offer. "That sounds excellent, but the truth is I can't afford the airfare. The house has busted the bank."

Our friend paused again and then said, "I have quite a few frequent flyer miles. In fact, I'm sure I have enough for two round trips. So why don't you be my guest?"

The offer was so generous, it was difficult for Patrick to hear and even more so to accept. He began to say, "No thanks, there's so much to do." At this point I stepped in.

"Are you crazy?" I asked. "There's nothing that can't wait. So why don't you go?"

It came as such a shock that it took a bit of persuasion, but eventually Patrick was able graciously to accept the gift, both from our friend and from the Universe.

Guidance and support are there for those who have the eyes to see, the ears to hear, and the heart to accept what the Universe has to offer.

DO YOU WANT GUIDANCE?

Often the greatest obstacle to Principle Number Five is our own attachment to false ideas and preset expectations and a love and attachment to our own comfortable, familiar misery. At least once a month I encounter a client who asks for guidance but really is just sounding off, uninterested in any solutions whatsoever.

Recently I met with a woman, Maureen, who was in a miserable marriage. She said her husband was a hardworking man, made a good living, was faithful, and took a great interest in their children. The problem was that he was negative and controlling, and they butted heads on every issue. Whenever she said "go" he said "stop." Whenever she said "yes" he said "no." They were a modern-day version of the Bickersons, a fictitious radio couple of the thirties known for their incessant arguing.

Maureen was quite animated as she recounted her frustrations with her husband. She told he how hard she worked, only to be criticized for being lazy. She told me what a beautiful home she had created, only to be told she spent too much money. She told me how much attention she lavished on her children, only to be told she spoiled them. Her marriage boiled down to her heroic efforts to win the support and approval of someone unwilling to give it. It did sound miserable.

What's more, her efforts were focused completely on what her husband expected rather than on what she wanted for herself. This left her bitter and angry. She wanted to know if I saw any change coming in her miserable life.

"Maureen," I suggested, "change begins with you. You need to see a therapist to sort out your need to please such a disagreeable man."

"Oh, I've thought of that," she snapped, "but John will have a fit if I spend money on therapy."

I paused, then said, "Well, perhaps you can attend codependent meetings, which are free."

"Well, that's occurred to me, too, but I can't do that, either John would be angry with me if I weren't at home with the kids in the evening."

I paused again and said, "Maureen, you are an adult woman and you sound as if John is your father. Have you considered marriage counseling?"

"Good heavens, no," she balked. "He'd never go for that."

Exasperated, I made one final suggestion. "Why don't, you read a book called *Getting the Love You Want* by Harville Hendricks? It has practical suggestions for ways to improve a sour marriage, and I'm sure you would get something gout of it." "Well..." She hesitated. "Please, write the name of it down, but I don't know when I'll find time to read it. Do you see anything else for me?"

"No," I said, smiling. "Only more of the same."

I wrote down the book title and handed it to her. She told me a few more irritating stories about John and then said with a sigh, "I was really hoping you'd tell me something more hopeful than this. Oh well. Maybe next year."

After she left I noticed that the paper I had given her with the book title was still sitting on my desk. Evidently she didn't really want guidance. She wanted to be rescued, and that I couldn't do.

SPIRITUAL GUIDANCE IS SUBTLE

Spirit is subtle and often overlooked by those who aren't paying attention. If you are preoccupied with brain-rumbling angers, fears, rash judgments, closed-minded opinions—you are going to miss your cues. True guidance will rest lightly in your mind, like a feather, and true guidance requires a calm, receptive mind to be intercepted.

Your part at this stage in manifesting your dream is to create the habit of being in a calm, receptive state of mind or at least to start moving in that direction. So slow down, breathe deeply, relax, and trust that guidance is on the way. It will be good for you health as well.

Principle Number Five guides you along the way to your dream, one clue at a time. All you have to do is be open for the clues, expect they will be there, trust them as they show up, and act on them when they do.

When you come to Principle Number Five, you enter the land of wonder—"I wonder how the Universe will open up to my dream?" Know that it will, and look forward to being surprised at how. It will amaze you. It will delight you. And you can be sure, above all, that the way your soul leads you will be so incredibly simple that you never could have thought of it in advance!

When you apply Principle Number Five, life becomes less of a struggle. This is where each day is filled with the potential to delight you. This is where you will begin to feel the support of Divine guidance. You will learn at this point that you don't *make* magic happen—but if only you allow it, there is magic abounding everywhere.

Principle Number Five heals the heart, takes away fear, and shifts your attention back to its rightful focus: your soul. It removes the burden of figuring things out. It saves you the wear and tear of worry, obsessing, fear, and frustration. It will bring you to a wonderful state of inner calm.

As you practice Principle Number Five, look and listen with full awareness—not to others, but to your intuition. Keep your mind clear and quiet. Meditate every morning. Pray every night. Ask freely and openly for what you need. You never know if you might not be asking an angel. And know that it is the Fifth Principle of the Universe that you can fully expect to be guided at this point in your journey.

You've earned it!

PRACTICING THE FIFTH PRINCIPLE

LISTENING FOR GUIDANCE

- Start every day, before you open your eyes, with a prayer asking Divine spirit for guidance.

- Take a ten-minute meditation break instead of a coffee break.

- Write a letter to your Higher Self and ask your soul for directions in finding the way to your dream. Then write a letter from your soul back to you, telling you what to. (Try this—it works!)

- *Wonder* instead of wander through your day.

- Practice being flexible and spontaneous. Follow your impulses instead of shooing them away like flies. Whenever possible, ask out loud for help and guidance—in the shower, in the car, in the bathroom, whenever you are not alone. (Better yet, *whenever* you need guidance, alone or not!)

- Whenever you have an urge to ask for help, do so. You may be talking to an angel.

GET OUT OF YOUR HEAD

Avoid intellectualizing your future. (This is mostly chewing gum for your fears anyway.) Remember that you are a spiritual creator and that your soul knows where to lead you and is doing so now.

Quiet down. Practice silence whenever possible. Eliminate background noise. Shut off the radio and the TV. Don't fill your mind with useless opinion disguised as fact. Become contemplative and receptive to spirit, as a habit. Meditate and relax.

MEDITATION

Find a comfortable, quiet place to sit, and gently close your eyes. Notice the difference that simply closing your eyes brings about.

Now take three slow, deep breaths, allowing yourself to settle down and connect with whatever is supporting you. With each breath you exhale, allow yourself to feel solid and one with the earth. Continue to focus on your breathing until you are in a quiet, balanced state.

Now imagine gazing into a crystal blue sky. Imagine yourself dreaming, drifting, relaxed, and peaceful as you gaze at the clouds drifting by.

As you allow yourself to mentally drift, imagine a radiant light pouring down upon you, covering your body and soul in a warm, loving glow. Feeling secure and at ease, allow yourself to become more and more relaxed with each breath you exhale as this loving light fills your entire being.

Imagine this light resting in your heart. Let your attention gently slip away from your thoughts and follow the light into your heart. There you will hear a loving voice that resonates deep within you. Relax. Breathe. Listen.

This is the voice of your Higher Self, gently guiding you toward your Heart's Desire. Know that this inner voice is available to you at any time.

This voice is all-knowing, loving and powerful, competent and wise, safe, subtle. Quietly focus your attention onto this inner guidance and let your awareness become totally receptive to following your higher guidance.

Listen quietly for a few moments.

When you are ready, slowly open your eyes.

REVIEW

If you are able to follow these steps to Principle Number Five—celebrate! Then move on to Principle Number Six.

If not, go back and review Principles One through Four.

PRINCIPLE NUMBER SIX

Choose to Support Your Dream with Love

As you progress to Principle Number Six, you are completing the second phase of creativity. In this final step you actually begin to control how you want to manifest your dream. At this point in the process you choose *how* you want your Heart's Desire to happen.

Principle Number Six is about choice and action. As you move through the Principles you come to realize that no matter what you want to create, whether it's a new love relationship or a new job, it will require choice and action form you. As long as you live on earth, no matter what you want to create, you have to *do* something to create it. Even if that something is sitting in a cave meditating, you have to get to the cave and then meditate.

Principle Number Six states: "Choose to support your dream with love." This Principle focuses your attention on two separate points. This Principle focuses your attention on two separate points. The first point is to *choose* to support your dream. The second point is to do so "with love".

It sounds obvious enough, yet so many people do not make day-to-day choices that will support their dream, let alone support it with love. So often we say we want to create something, yet we choose behaviors, thoughts, and actions that actually sabotage our success and support just the opposite. I believe Principle Number Six is the heart of your Heart's Desire. When you choose to make loving decisions that agree with what you desire, you attract your Heart's Desire directly to you.

I had a client named Robert, a jovial, pleasant, but very overweight man whose dream was to lose seventy-five pounds. He envisioned himself svelte and made a collage of photos from a time when he was thin. Yet in spite of his desire and imaginings, when it came right down to it he chose to eat fattening "nonfoods" like cheesecake, chips, and doughnuts, topped off by a sixteen-ounce steak. He played games with himself over what he chose to eat, reasoning, "I was good all week, so I just had to have a tiny reward." Then he'd binge on some fattening food, putting back on any pounds he had lost.

He would then be so unhappy over his lack of success that he would eat even more. Principle Number Six was the one he needed to apply when he came to the Heart's Desire workshop.

He said, "My goal is to lose seventy-five pounds. I *have* to stop bingeing on food and *force* myself to stay on my diet!" All very loveless propositions as far as I could see.

"First of all, Robert," I said, "you must examine how you use your power of choice."

"What do you mean?" he asked.

"Well, anytime you make a choice in your life you are motivated either by love or by fear. When you are motivated by love, the effort comes easily and is rewarding. When you are motivated by fear, the effort is difficult, burdensome, and usually ineffective. Saying 'have to' is motivating yourself with fear."

"So that's why it's so difficult!" he responded.

"When you make a choice with fear, some part of you rebels. The reality is that unless you bring love to your choices and make ones that support your dream, you are going to fail. In your case, Robert, you must choose to love yourself and your body enough to nurture yourself in a healthy way. Your choice has to center first on loving yourself, not on fearing being fat."

"In other words," he said, "I should choose strawberries instead of cheesecake."

"Exactly," I said. "Choices such as these may require discipline on your part, but don't confuse discipline with punishment. Discipline means to learn, not to hurt. If you use discipline to learn to nurture yourself in a loving way, then perhaps you will succeed.

"The key word is enthusiasm. When you choose to love yourself with *enthusiasm*, you invite in a host of Divine support. Do you know what the word 'enthusiasm' means? It means 'of the gods.' When you are enthusiastic, you are working with Divine support. No matter what we are doing, an enthusiastic choice behind it makes a big difference."

Robert decided to stop resisting the support he needed from himself. He made up his mind to be enthusiastic about his dream. He began making choices that supported what he wanted. He went from choosing fatty to choosing fresh foods and began to cook at home instead of frequenting restaurants, as was his previous habit. He began to see that equating fatty snack foods with loving himself was a lie. Instead of being angry with his body, he began to see it through loving eyes.

It was hard at first, but slowly he began to eat in an authentically loving way. As he laughingly put it, "I decided to eat *food* for a change. It's a whole new world!"

Recognizing that he had many choices in how he supported his desire, he not only gradually changed his eating habits, he also took up skiing on a NordicTrack machine. Robert said he was "skiing to thinness!"

He also realized that behind his overeating was a desire for nurturing and support. He joined an addiction recovery program for his overeating, where he found enthusiasm, support, and love from people who understood his problem.

When I saw Robert last, he was fifty pounds lighter and planning to go on a cross-country ski trip with a new club he had joined. He looked like someone who had clearly chosen to support what he wanted, and he was *loving* it!

The power of choice is the catalyst toward your dream. Your choices begin to turn the wheels of manifestation.

If you are not in the habit of making self-loving choices, you may need some practice.

A client named Kate came to see me for a reading. Her desire was to be in a loving relationship, yet she chose to be involved with a man who was critical, selfish, noncommittal, and verbally abusive. She wanted to know if this man could ever be her Heart's Desire.

"Kate, you desire a loving relationship, but you choose an abusive one," I answered. "This man's impact on you is as poisonous as arsenic. I see that your experience of him actually makes you ill. How *do* you feel when you are with him?"

"I never thought about it before," she said, "but now that I do, he does give me migraine headaches."

"Can you see that your Heart's Desire is not possible with this man—in fact, is not possible until you make loving choices to support it?"

"How?" Kate asked. "I'm not sure what you mean."

"Well, you can start by choosing to avoid men who sicken you. You are not only with the wrong partner, he is occupying the place in your life that is intended for your true love."

"But I get lonely..." she said.

"And you are afraid there's no one else," I finished.

She admitted, "You're right."

"Kate, you must realize that making choices from fear will only create fear. Try making choices that reflect a loving attitude toward yourself. Your choices need to agree with your desire. If you desire to experience love, choose to love yourself enough to create that kind of experience."

Kate left, pondering her options.

Bit by bit she began to understand how her choices were self-defeating. Every date with her boyfriend became harder and harder for her to tolerate. She began to choose not to see him when he asked and felt very strong when she did this. Eventually other men started to ask her out, and very thoughtfully she chose to accept only those offers that were genuinely comfortable for her.

Kate is not yet in the relationship she wants, but she is learning about love (finally) toward herself, a feeling more satisfying than any she had felt before.

Kate's conflict between choice and desire is very common. It occurs when you choose out of fear instead of love. When you choose from fear, you do not believe you can have what you want. You believe you can have only what you get (which is fear). It's a vicious cycle.

It happens when you want a better job but choose to keep the one you have for fear there aren't better ones.

It happens when you desire an adventure but choose to stay in a rut for fear you won't be safe or secure.

Choice creates, whether from fear or love. You can choose either way. Here's what happened to one man who chose love over fear.

Raul called to ask for a reading several years ago. A soft-spoken and elegant thirty-two-year-old gay man from South America, he was an artist by training who was obliged to work as a busboy in a restaurant to survive. When he came to my office be brought a letter with him, which he threw down on the table.

He said, "Hold this and use your intuition to tell me if it will accomplish what I want."

I picked up the letter and felt its passion, but I also felt rage, scorn, and fear. I knew he wanted to send a message, but it was a misdirected one.

"Raul," I said, "this letter is scathing, and in its present form I'm afraid its message will fall on deaf ears."

He looked frustrated and disappointed. "It's a letter to the president," he said, "asking him to open up more money to AIDS research. I have seven close friends, and each one of us has tested HIV-positive. And not one of us has the money to secure the medical care we need. This is a very serious problem, not only for me, but for all HIV-positive people, and I feel I must try to do something."

He was totally focused on his desire to stimulate funding for AIDS research, but his choices were full of hostility, which would get him nowhere. My reading pointed Raul in another direction.

"Raul, your gifts and strengths are those of an artist. I see you opening an art gallery that you can also serve as a public platform to educate people about AIDS. This is the way you will be heard and respected by the community."

His eyes opened wide in disbelief. "That would be my greatest dream, but the reality is that I am a political refugee and very poor. In my country I was a curator in a museum, but here I pour water and coffee in a restaurant. I can barely afford my bills, not to mention the fears I face with my health. Though I would love nothing more, how can I possibly do this?"

"Even though you work in a restaurant for the moment," I said, "you are still who you are—an artist. Don't lose sight of that. Don't worry about how to be who you are. Simply choose to let people know who you are, and let the Universe take care of the rest."

Raul left, enthused but incredulous. He chose to follow the suggestions of Principle Number Six and began, little by little, to speak of his dreams more openly. Within four months a customer who frequented the restaurant and had listened to Raul spontaneously offered to back his dream. Together they formed an art gallery, a perfect venue for all of Raul's most heartfelt desires.

That was seven years ago. Raul has just recently moved out of his original space and into an even more desirable location. He has gained local and national acclaim for both his gallery and his vision in his campaign for AIDS sufferers. He went from refugee status to respected community spokesperson, gaining the support and enthusiasm of significant political leaders in his city.

All this occurred when Raul chose to remember who he was and to love himself and his purpose enough to share it with others. Having done so, he is now living the full expression of his Heart's Desire.

This is a perfect example of the attracting powers of Principle Number Six. As for his health, all seven of his friends have since died, but Raul, though not in perfect health, still feels good and is able to do what he loves. He said that soon after he discovered he was HIV-positive, he decided to live his life as a loving, peaceful man. He is certain that this choice has had a very positive effect on his ability to slow the course of his disease.

When you choose to bring love and enthusiasm to your Heart's Desire, the whole process takes on a magical and healing quality. You stop hitting a brick wall. You stop going against the grain. You stop dragging yourself through your life like deadweight. When you introduce love and enthusiasm into your Heart's Desire, you rise up, almost like stepping onto a magic carpet, and begin to float gracefully toward what you want—not effortlessly, but gracefully. It will remove your obstacles and help you find your balance, as my own daughters demonstrated so well to me last summer.

We had just moved into a new neighborhood where we could give them a little more freedom than they had had in our previous (and slightly more dangerous) Chicago neighborhood. The first thing they wanted to do with this newfound freedom was to learn to ride their bicycles without training wheels, an option they hadn't had before because of their lack of opportunity to practice. So one day we removed both sets of training wheels and took them out to the sidewalk.

Sonia, my seven-year-old, was determined. I could feel that every cell in her body *intended* to catch up to the other kids on the block that very day! Sure enough, fifteen minutes into her first attempt without the training wheels, she took off, rolling victoriously down the street. We all cheered wildly until I turned and found her six-year-old sister, Sabrina, in a disheveled slump on the ground, sobbing.

"Sabrina, what's wrong?" I asked.

"I hate Sonia! She can ride without her training wheels and I can't." Tears were rolling down her face. "Now everyone will laugh at me and call me a baby."

"Now come on, Sabrina. She's a year older. You just need some practice."

"Other kids on this block are only *five* and they can ride their bikes without training wheels. I hate them! Especially Sonia!" She was devastated and feeling very left behind with her sister now halfway down the block for the third time. She was inconsolable.

Patrick stepped in. "Beans, don't cry. Relax. I'll teach you to ride. Come on."

She dried her tears and took his hand, still feeling very sorry for herself and angry with the other kids. Patrick put her up on her bike, gave her a running push, and... *crash!* She was down just as soon as he let go of her. Crying, Sabrina got up, shaking and upset.

Patrick put her right back on the bike. He gave her a second running push. Once again she crashed and wiped out immediately.

By now Sonia was nearly flying past us, yelling, "Sabrina, look at me!"

Sabrina just glared at her. Feeling her own prospects of success were nil, she started slipping back into despair, tears rolling down her face.

"Beans," Patrick said, "stop being angry and upset with the others and think instead about how much you'd love to ride your bike. That's the secret to learning to ride."

Sabrina sniffled and listened.

"Let's try it," Patrick said. "Imagine each one of your feet is full of love, and then push all that love into the pedals as hard as you can! Focus on where you want to when you do this, and say out loud, 'I love riding my bike! I love riding my bike!' Don't focus on anything else, okay? Now, are you ready?"

Sabrina was intrigued with the idea. Half giggling and half suspicious, she said, "Okay, I'll try it." She got up onto her bike, still tentative, but saying, "I love my..."

Oops! Over she went.

"See yourself riding easily. Love riding your bike even more, Sabrina!" Patrick yelled. "Focus straight ahead when you say it."

She got back up and tried again. "I *love* riding my bike. I *love* riding my bike," she said more determinedly this time, traveling a full fifteen feet before crashing.

Encouraged, we all squealed with delight and cheered her on. Even the other kids gathered around, wanting to see her go.

Patrick urged, "Do it again, Beans. This time, *really* love riding your bike! I know you can do it. Push all that love into each pedal the best you can and focus on where you are going. Just stay calm and give it your very best try."

Delighted and surprised at her progress, Sabrina jumped on the bike once again, now laughing and screaming, "I *love* riding my bike! I *love* riding my bike!" She shoved each foot down as hard as she could, intent on where she wanted to go—and *whoosh!* She was off!

The kids roared. Each push on the pedal was magic. Pedaling harder and harder, she was loving that bike all the way down the block. Finding that magic place of balance, she sailed down the street like the wind, riding the magic of love.

Bringing love into your choices as you work toward your dream brings in the support of the Universe. What is difficult when approached with resistance becomes a breeze when approached with loving enthusiasm. This is because when you are enthusiastic and loving, Divine support will join you. As the saying goes, "All the world loves a lover."

Principle Number Six is about power. Not the kind of power that erupts out of the personal ego, but the kind that gracefully flows through you when you tap into the loving support of the Universe.

CREATE YOUR DREAM, NOT SOMEONE ELSE'S

One of the most common arguments I hear for making choices that run contrary to people's goals is, "I can't choose what I want because I can't afford to." People are very good at fearfully creating situations that they do not want and then letting their creations hold them prisoner.

Marvin's desire was to be a writer, but he chose to go into business with his brother-in-law selling insurance instead. Needless to say, Marvin was unhappy with his choice in spite of the fact that the business was quite profitable. He kept at it for ten years, ignoring the truth that each year be he became more and more frustrated.

Finally Marvin reached a point where he hated to go to work. That's when he called me for a reading.

During our conversation Marvin told me that he felt guilty about his desire to quit the business because it made money. He also felt guilty because his brother-in-law depended upon him so much, and quitting could hurt Marvin's sister. If he quit, he thought, it would ruin them all financially, a prospect he didn't want to face.

To ease his guilt he overcompensated by working all the more, which only buried him deeper and deeper in the job. By the time Marvin came to see me, he was under an avalanche of obligation and feeling very trapped. And no wonder. His head and his heart were completely at war, and his choices were completely out of sync with his desire.

"Marvin," I said, "your choices do not support your dream in any way. They support your brother-in-law's dream instead and are totally fueled by your fears. In order to create what you want, you need to respond to *your* heart's calling, not his."

Marvin couldn't accept that fact. "If I do what I love, I'll devastate my sister, put my brother-in-law out of business, and go broke."

I didn't see the same scenario and did not feel his family was nearly as dependent on him as he chose to believe. I tried to tell him that he overrated his importance and underestimated both the flexibility of his family and his own ability to make a living in creative ways, but he stopped me short.

"You don't know what you're talking about. You don't know my sister. They couldn't possibly survive without me, so how could I have one peaceful moment to write?"

Marvin was obviously not able to see any other possibility than to remain rigidly attached to his fears. He left as miserable as when he came, in spite of my effort to convince him that he did have options that wouldn't hurt anyone.

Eighteen months later Marvin came back for another reading, and this time he was furious. Apparently his sister and brother-in-law had suddenly informed him of their plans to move to Montana at the end of the summer without including him in the decision.

Marvin told me, "They said I seemed so deeply involved in the business that they thought I wouldn't mind."

I wanted to smile, but I didn't, "Marvin, you should be thrilled," I said. "Now you can get on to your dreams."

But Marvin wasn't thrilled. He was too upset over the wasted years he had spent trying to take care of his family. The truth was, their happiness had nothing to do with him, and he wasn't responsible for them in spite of his beliefs. But his responsibility to himself had been seriously neglected, and this was the real root of this anger.

Marvin and his brother-in-law decided to sell the business and split the proceeds. Meanwhile Marvin took a job at a not-for-profit newsletter and at the same time began to work on his first novel. He had saved a fair amount of money over the years, which supplemented his now substantially diminished income. He grudgingly admitted that he was happier to be out of that job, although he was still fuming over his brother-in-law's indifference to the sacrifices he had made for their business. I suggested he see a therapist to work through some of his anger, which he agreed to do.

A year later I heard from Marvin again. This time he told he was taking a scriptwriting course and occasionally selling a jingle or two for radio. When I asked if he felt any better about his brother-in-law he said, "It's ancient history. I'm enjoying my life so much these days that I've decided to let it go."

Better late than never.

Have you ever fallen into this trap? Are you taking responsibility for others' dreams while neglecting your own? Choices such as these usually backfire, and if you choose to be the saint or the martyr, I must warn you it's a thankless job. People don't appreciate the sacrifices you make if they are greater than you can freely give.

It's better to be honest and trust that people can adjust their needs if they must when you allow yourself to follow your heart. They may complain, but they can and will work things out. You will help people far more by being true to yourself and living your dream than by being angry, bitter, and resentful.

Principle Number Six is about love, not about sentimentality, caretaking, martyrdom, sainthood, or victimization, which many of us have been led to believe is love. We have been trained that putting others before ourselves is an expression of love, but usually it isn't. It is an expression of fear.

I have heard these objections to Principle Number Six:

"It will upset the status quo."

"My kids need me."

"My partner won't like it."

"The job comes first."

"Who will take care of things?"

"My routine will change."

Et cetera, et cetera, et cetera. When you choose to put everything before your Heart's Desire, you are choosing out of fear (even if it's a well-intentioned fear) to stay in the familiar patterns of suffering and lack. Principle Number Six confronts those habits and helps bring you back into balance.

I realize we live with others, and part of life is to be responsible and accountable where needed, such as to our children, families, and friends, especially if they are young or sick. I am not talking about becoming self-absorbed and walking away from true responsibilities.

What I am talking about is choosing a balanced path, a way to fit your dreams into your life instead of sacrificing them for others. If your life is full of "have to" and "should" obligations, take a look at your choices. Do you choose to lovingly support yourself? If not, try changing your perspective on what it means to love. After all, Jesus Christ said, "Love your neighbor as yourself." And as for helping others, he said, "Get up and walk," not, "I'll carry you."

Principle Number Six is about becoming fully responsible to your dreams and desires and making them happen lovingly for yourself instead of hoping for rescue.

LOVING CHOICES ATTRACT ABUNDANCE

Often people prevent themselves from choosing what they want for fear that there won't be the necessary money or support to allow it.

The Principles of Creativity teach that all creation comes from the limitless supply of the Universe. Remember, all things flow from the Universal source, and you can tap into this source when you apply Principle Number Six to your dream.

If you have difficulty experiencing the support of the Universe through your own choices, then make it your choice to seek out the community of other supportive voices. Fortunately these are abundant—addiction groups, creativity gatherings, volunteer groups, spiritual communities, group therapy, even group sports and recreation. Principle Number Six is essentially about support, and the way to tap into the limitless support of the Universe is to lovingly *choose* to be supported, in every possible way.

Here's how Principle Number Six can solve this dilemma.

Over the past ten years, when Patrick and I would go out to dinner we frequently chose a particular restaurant and asked to be seated in Jacob's section. The reason was that when Jacob waited on us, he did his job with such loving enthusiasm that I was a pleasure to be served by him. And every time he waited on us, we gave him a very generous tip because he was so enjoyable to be around. He was as appealing as the food.

Over the years, Jacob confided that it was his goal to move to Italy and open a Chicago-style hot dog stand. "I have no money or experience in business," he'd say, "but I would *love* to try it. It would be such a dream!"

Each time we saw him he had either just returned from vacationing in Italy or was planning on going there in the near future. He also told us he was taking Italian lessons and was getting better all the time. No doubt about it, Italy was his passion.

The last time we went out to dinner, Jacob was gone. He had quite his job and gone off to Italy to fulfill his dream. Another waiter informed us that Jacob had saved over $100,000 in tips because he was so popular.

"What a lucky guy," he said.

I knew that there really was no luck involved. It was his loving and enthusiastic attitude toward his customers that took him to Rome, the city of the gods.

I'm sure he'll fit right in.

Let me tell you the story of another client who chose to embrace Principle Number Six.

Grace is a very creative and spiritual woman who has lived in many places and done many fascinating things. She has been a painter, a writer, a musician, a product designer, and a chef. In spite of these talents, however, when I met her she had a subsistence job in a flower shop. Her life was burdened with debt, and her sense of purpose was unfulfilled. When she attended our workshop she expressed to us that it had been her Heart's Desire for some time to become a spiritual healer in the arts of reiki and shamanism, but that she feared she would not be able to support herself.

I suggested that she apply Principle Number Six to her Heart's Desire, which is also the Principle of attraction.

"When you work with love you draw others to you," I said. "Embrace this truth. The reason for this is that love is the highest vibration on earth. When you work with love people feel it, are helped by it, and return to it. It's a positive vibration that draws people naturally into its sphere. Those who love what they do emote that love through their work, and people are drawn toward their energy. That's why love is the best marketing tool around. Because it is so attractive, it pulls right to you what you need."

Grace did decide to follow her heart and embrace her chosen vocation. As she said, "It feels so right I can't resist. I love doing this work."

She started out with just a couple of clients a month, still keeping her "regular" job as a florist. But in just a matter of months the word was out in the community that people were being greatly helped, and calls for appointments started coming in.

In a short eight months she had to let go of her regular job because she couldn't fit it into her schedule! By the end of the first year her practice had exploded. She was booked solid for a month at a time. In the second year she paid off her old debts, moved to a beautiful apartment, and was asked to be an outside consultant for a holistic health center as an intuitive diagnostician. By the end of the second year she was struggling to find time off for relaxation because she had attracted so many clients. Each day her abilities expanded, and every experience with a client was a miracle of healing in itself.

Principle Number Six drew in more work and abundance than Grace ever could have guessed. Above all, she was fulfilled in her Heart's Desire. Healing was her purpose, and she loved living it! Choosing to work with Principle Number Six, expressing love and enthusiasm in what she did, attracted all that she required and more.

Because of this fulfillment, Grace's material needs lessened as well. She felt filled up with Universal love, and her physical wants greatly diminished. In working with Principle Number Six, she was supported beyond what she had every imagined, and in many more ways than money.

Jenny was a single flight attendant in her fifties. It was Jenny's Heart's Desire to meet a wealthy man and get married, yet when she talked about men she would almost seethe with contempt. Much of her negative attitude came from her many disappointments in being "the other woman" in several married men's lives over the years. She felt cheated, ripped off, and used.

"Men are so selfish and such liars. I *hate* them!" she cried.

Yet Jenny wanted to get married. Hmmm, I thought.

"Jenny it sounds as though you have been very hurt and wounded by all these rejections. What is it about men that you are so attracted to?"

"Honestly, I don't love men," she said in a moment of truth. "I love the security of their money. My income isn't great, and job security as a flight attendant is nonexistent. I worry all the time about being old, alone and poor."

I said, "Well, why don't you change your goal from one of hoping a man will marry you as a means of achieving security to one of making money yourself as a way to feel secure, since that's your true Heart's Desire?"

"That would be a switch," Jenny mused. "I'd love to make my own money. I'm sick of depending on men to feel secure. I never do, anyway. But how can I make any real money at my age? I don't have any skills. Nice idea, but unrealistic. No, a man is the only solution."

"Jenny, your problem is that you won't take financial responsibility for your dream and get the skills you need. Why don't you take an investment course?" I proposed. "I bet you would love it. Just try it before you decide if it's realistic or not. You never know."

Jenny left unconvinced. She chose instead to have a brief affair with a younger man and suffered through another humiliating rejection. That was the last straw. She finally made up her mind to choose another way to financial security, a way she might truly embrace with enthusiasm.

Jenny enrolled in a basic investment course at a local adult education program. She enjoyed learning about stocks, bonds, mutual funds, and investment strategies and found that she had a talent for it (due perhaps in part to listening to all her lovers over the years). In six months she had set up a modest portfolio and had secured a part-time job at a local investment firm, where she worked between flights.

Jenny got so involved in making money that she forgot all about pursuing men. And when she was asked out, she found she was much more discriminating. She wasn't "investing" in a man anymore. She was having a lot more fun investing in herself. The security she was searching for was finally becoming available to her. She loved building her fortune and seeing herself as a competent money manager and professional.

In Jenny's case, her choices had been misdirected. She chose men to get security. When she decided to direct her choice to gaining knowledge of money itself, literally without the middle *man*, she realized her true Heart's Desire—the security of self-reliance and the joy of turning a profit!

Jenny found her Heart's Desire through her own efforts. The choice of working from love, for yourself and for your goal, can result in miracles. What feels impossible will begin to feel manageable. What was closed off to you will open. The Principle of love is the Principle of true magic.

The magic of love will attract support. When you work from love, you will attract enthusiasm. Others will get excited about you and what you are doing and want to help. Wherever there is real love, real enthusiasm, there is also the grace of God. People cannot resist the energy of love because, deep down, that is all any of us ever want to feel. And when we do, we like it and want to be around it, cheering it on. That is the secret of charisma—loving what you are doing so much that there is no drag, no resistance, no negativity, in your energy field. You become a clear white beam of light. All the people you touch feel the energy around you, and they'll cheer you on and light up the way.

WHAT IF YOU GET STUCK ON THE FENCE?

I have had students who have a clear idea of what their hearts desire, and they even use behaviors to support them, but they fail to find the necessary love and enthusiasm to energize their choices and their process.

I met Sharon when I was teaching a course in Harrisburg, Pennsylvania. She was a gifted, even celebrated, psychic who had been written about in books. But though she loved the work she did, she did not have the self-esteem to ask payment for her services and so worked at a job she despised. Even though on weekends and evenings she was inundated with requests for spiritual help, she kept telling herself she had to keep her job at the telephone company and had to do her psychic work at no charge.

This "have to" thinking drained her day and night. In the end she worked constantly. (I call it the "chronic exhale" mode—give, give, give, never receive.) This thinking stemmed from being the oldest in a puritanical religious family that focused on self-denial and suffering as a spiritual path. She had a hard enough time accepting being psychic, so she made it spiritually "okay" by giving her work away.

This went on for years. Sharon developed chronic fatigue syndrome and became very depressed. "But I have to..." was her persistent stance in spite of these obvious signs of soulful decline. Two months prior to receiving her pension for twenty-five years of have-to service, Sharon was laid off. After another month of have-to psychic handouts, she was involved in a head-on car crash.

Obviously the Universe was trying to tell her something she wasn't willing to hear. Sharon ended up in the hospital in a coma and recalls vividly being visited by three angels who came to her bedside to tell her she must do her psychic work and trust that the Universe would support her. Eventually she awoke from the coma and slowly her body recovered, but she still suffered from "have to" thinking.

"I know that my purpose is psychic counseling, but something inside me does not feel worthy to receive support. I just wish I could earn a living doing this."

I told Sharon that she needed to open her heart and allow the love she expressed to return to her full circle. I shared with her a Chinese proverb about love that *I* love: "When you are willing to receive what you are willing to give, and when you are willing to give what you are willing to receive, then you understand love."

Sharon's eyes sparkled when she heard that concept. Learning to receive as an act of love was new to her. I left Sharon contemplating new beginnings.

If you are stuck on the fence, unable to lovingly support your own path, then perhaps you are frightened at the notion of receiving. You may feel vulnerable if you open your heart and allow yourself to feel support if you have not experienced this before. This is most often true if you come from an abusive family or have abusive relationships. Asking and believing that the Universe loves you *as* you, and supports you, can be very frightening if you have experienced just the opposite from the people you love.

If you are stuck on the fence about choosing to love and support your dream, see your predicament for what it is and seek support from those who have been there. Join a self-help group such as AA or Al-Anon, or seek the guidance of a therapist, a spiritual counselor, and supportive and safe friends. Your greatest obstacle to creating Heart's Desire may be isolation, and what you need is the love and community of people who want you to succeed. Doing this will energize you and get you off the fence.

Jesus once said, "Wherever there are three or more gathering in my name, I will be there also." This means recognizing the power of others to help you. Community creates the synergy for miracles to happen.

Manifesting your dream requires choices from you, but if the choice flows from your heart and is undertaken with love and enthusiasm, it will be a pleasure. And it *will* attract support. As the word "enthusiasm" denotes, it will be infused with the energy of the gods.

Change your "have to" thinking to "love to" thinking. Go about the work of your creativity with a sense of pleasure. For one day, practice saying "I'd love to" to every request made of you. Notice any difference in the way things go?

When I was a child we did our family chores while singing. We always started out with a rousing chorus of "Whistle While You Work," then continued with every Broadway musical, Beatles tune, and Tom Jones song we could think of. As we worked we laughed a lot, performed, and generally had a good time.

On laundry day we folded the socks for all seven kids into sock balls. One at a time, each kid would stand up and sing a song. If whoever was singing forgot the words or went off-key, that kid was pelted with sock balls. The one with the most sock balls had to put away all the remaining laundry. What could have been an endless menial job became our favorite weekend event.

Enthusiasm is contagious. In no time, every kid on the block wanted to be at our house on laundry day. Half the time it was one of our tone-deaf neighbor kids putting away our laundry, but no one seemed to mind. The fun was worth the work.

Life changes when you stop thinking and saying "I have to." Even though it sometimes appears that choices are few, know that there are always ways to leave a bad situation for a better one. Many of us get into the rut of being comfortable in our misery and become so accustomed to abuse or frustration that it actually begins to feel normal.

The truth is that suffering is not your only choice. You can always find a way to support your dreams if you are willing to take the risk of leaving the familiar. You may be required to think creatively in order to change, which may not be your habit, but ask yourself: What would I do if the troubling relationship or situation were to vanish tomorrow?

The answer, of course, is that you would adapt by making new choices. And when you consciously choose to support your progress, all the Universe will be behind you.

We all come to earth to create. It is our purpose. When you infuse your will to create with real love and enthusiasm, the effort becomes a pleasure. People who work with love attract it into their lives. People who work with enthusiasm bring it out in others. Magical thinking does not mean manipulative thinking. It does not mean getting out of the work involved, escaping the necessary steps to your dream. It means working from your true self, your soul, and being authentic about what you must do to create your dream.

Remember, Principle Number Six is the heart of your Heart's Desire. Whatever you want, *love* to choose at least one action toward that dream every single day. If you do, you will attract, as lovers do, all the love and enthusiasm of the Universe.

PRACTICING THE SIXTH PRINCIPLE

THE CHOICE IS YOURS

Now it's time for you to choose what you will do with enthusiasm to support your Heart's Desire. For example:

- If you want to develop your artistic talents, choose to take an art class.
- If you want to lose weight, choose to eat healthful food and to enjoy physical activity.
- If you want to create a new relationship with someone, choose to smile, to enjoy meeting people, to say yes when asked to attend new functions.
- If you want to grow spiritually, choose to meditate, pray, and read inspirational material.
- If you want a new job, choose to write a résumé, tell people of your availability, look for new opportunities, read the want ads-*enthusiastically.*

You can always think of a way to support what you love if the desire is authentic and your aim is true.

EXERCISING DAILY LOVING CHOICES

Obtain a pocket-size daily planner. Every day make a notation of what choices you have made that day to support your Heart's Desire. Try to make a notation every day. If your desire is true, this should be a pleasure and each day will be more compelling than the last for working on your dream.

Note in big letters in your calendar the birthday of your dream, for if you do this, it will surely arrive.

(Note: If you cannot do this, or you skip many days in a row, then perhaps your desire is not true. Go back and review the First Principle.)

SEEING THE RESULTS

When you have followed through with your choices, complete the following:

YOUR DESIRE	
YOUR CHOICE TO SUPPORT IT	
THE OUTCOME	

MEDITATION

The meditation for this Principle is not only a meditation, but an affirmation. Repeat it several times a day.

Find a comfortable spot where you can sit quietly without being interrupted for at least five minutes. Close your eyes and begin to pay attention to your breath as it enters and then leaves your body.

Once you are in a calm, quiet state, silently repeat the following affirmation:

> *I choose only helpful actions,*
> *Exclusively supporting my Heart's Desire*
> *Mentally, emotionally, and physically.*

Focus your full attention on your Heart's Desire as you repeat this affirmation. Repeat it for five minutes; then, when you are ready, slowly open your eyes.

Note: The following technique can be used in a conscious state during the day. Each time you are tempted to behave in a way contrary to your dream, take a deep breath and say, out loud if possible:

> *I prefer to support my dream.*

Then change your action to a more supportive one.

Repeat these affirmations several times a day.

REVIEW

If you are able to follow these steps to Principle Number Six, then move on to Principle Number Seven.

If not, go back and review Principles One through Five.

PRINCIPLE NUMBER SEVEN

Surrender Control

The secret to creating your Heart's Desire is to use *all* of your energy, in every way possible, to bring about what you want. As you have seen, this is what Principles One through Six are all about. By focusing on following each Principle, step by step, you have been consciously aligning your energy so that it is directed *exclusively* toward your dream. In following each of these steps like a treasure map, you will be led straight to your special wish.

By working with these Principles as you have done so far, you are on your way to setting up the perfect conditions for Divine spirit to work through you, creating your dream. This is what Principle Number Seven is about—*allowing* Divine spirit to flow through you to do the work, instead of relying on your personal power to make it happen.

Once you have created the circumstances for magic and miracles to occur, then Principle Number Seven begins to operate. Essentially, this Principle instructs you to step aside and allow the Universe to take over and work its magic for a while. In other words, release your personal efforts to make things happen and put the process into God's hands. Doing this is the meaning of having faith.

Some people groan when they hear these words. For many people, having faith is no better than crossing their fingers, but nothing could be further from the truth. Notice that I have not mentioned faith until now. The reason is that until you create the perfect conditions for a miracle, there won't be one.

A farmer who hasn't planted seeds won't have a harvest. Nor will he if he doesn't tend his plants, water them, weed them, nurture them, protect them, and fertilize them. Yet it is important to realize that for all of his work, it is not the farmer who causes the seed to grow. It is the alchemy of the Universe, the spirit of Divine love working through the farmer, that grows the seed. The seed cannot sprout without the farmer's work, but when the farmer uses his energy to create a channel for Divine spirit to move into expression, a harvest is the natural outcome.

Principle Number Seven is the Principle of expectation. It is about allowing the Universe to orchestrate your miracle with confidence, knowing that set up the necessary conditions for the process to unfold.

This is what it means to have faith!

One of my favorite definitions of faith is "confidence in the future based on what you have done in the past." If you have followed Principles Number One through Six, you can move into faith gracefully. If you haven't done the work, however, faith will not do it for you.

TIMING IS EVERYTHING

Energy moves in cycles, and even dreams take time. The wisdom of Principle Number Seven is to know that time is also part of the creative process. As a matter of fact, timing is everything when it comes to a miracle, and placing your trust in the hands of God, timing and all, is what is called for now.

For example, Patrick and I shared a Heart's Desire to move into a larger house. We (I in particular) had been clearly focused on this goal for well over two years. In creating the perfect conditions, I read the real estate ads, drove around desirable neighborhoods, and talked to everyone who might have been helpful. I put our current house in order, ready to sell, and mentally moved out.

After six months of looking, I found what was *almost* the perfect house, and though it was not exactly what we wanted, I decided it was close enough. I wanted my Heart's Desire to happen *now* and had gotten tired of waiting for exactly the right thing to come along. I had become discouraged and feared that exactly what I wanted didn't exist or that we couldn't afford it, so I was willing to substitute less than my dream.

Though Patrick didn't agree with me, I was headstrong (a fault I still struggle with). I pushed my husband into bidding on the house. I knew I wasn't honoring Principle Number Seven, impatiently asserting my will over Divine will, but I ignored it. Patrick went along with me, even though his heart wasn't in it, mostly to appease me.

After many arguments, a lot of forcing and confrontation, and general bad feelings, we had to call off the deal. The truth was that the house was not only in bad repair, it was wrong for us. It was too small, did not have enough light, and wasn't laid out in a way that would suit our needs. In the end, only the neighborhood was right.

All along I could feel that I was using my will over Divine will to force a deal to come about. Ultimately the effort was exhausting and embarrassing, and it didn't work. We had no new house, everyone was angry, and I felt I was further from my dream than ever.

Yet I had to admit I was relieved. I knew that I had been trying to push everyone into accepting the house instead of waiting patiently for the right opportunity. I knew my ideas were wrong because they were so forced. I felt like Cinderella's stepsister trying to jam on a shoe that didn't fit. I gave up trying and decided to put my dream on the back burner for a while. I had done all I could, and any further efforts at that point felt like forcing open a locked door.

Eventually summer arrived. One night at a friend's barbecue, we began talking about houses. My friend suggested that we look in their neighborhood, which we had never considered before. Patrick and I toured the neighborhood and on one of our excursions fell in love with another house. We bid on it and were accepted. Everyone felt like a winner until the owner decided at the last moment that he wanted to rent the house to friends rather than sell to us. Once again the deal fell through.

Meanwhile, confident of our imminent move, we had sold our own house and were on the verge of moving out. We had to leave in a matter of weeks with no place to go. We were counseled by our realtor to "face reality" and rent a flat he had available. He assured us that what we wanted just wasn't possible. He knew the neighborhood well, and it wasn't going to happen right away. We would just have to wait it out.

Completely discouraged by our conversation with the realtor and the prospect of finding a house, I asked Divine will to take over, since things were not working out with me in charge. Moments later I sat down with the paper and opened the real estate section. To my amazement, leaping out from the page was a picture of exactly the kind of house I had dreamed of, an old Victorian in need of renovation. The best part was that this house was much less expensive, only a block away from our second choice in the "unavailable" neighborhood, and on a better street. Our realtor was shocked.

We made an offer that was accepted within hours. We gracefully closed on the house, renovated it in record time, and now are living comfortably in our new home.

The way things unfolded with our house reaffirmed for me the wisdom of following Principle Number Seven. When I ignored this Principle and impatiently tried to force my dream into being, I put myself and my family under a lot of stress. I wasted energy unnecessarily and didn't accomplish a thing. When I used Principle Number Seven and turned it over to the hidden forces of the Universe, it took six more months and a lot of flexibility, but we ended up with a far more wonderful outcome all around. The "shoe" slipped on perfectly, so to speak, and there was never an uncomfortable moment with the purchase.

Thank goodness I didn't get what I was forcing with my impatience! Instead the Universe delivered to us an even better version, gift-wrapped.

GO WITH THE FLOW

Principle Number Seven can be tough for people. It pushes us against our fears, confronts our need to control, and forces us to release into the hands of God the details of our innermost dreams and desires. It asks us to believe that all will turn out well in spite of appearances, which can be very challenging. When we encounter Principle Number Seven our faith is tested and so is our patience!

A client of mine, Sally, told me about her encounter with Principle Number Seven as she was preparing to see me for a reading.

"Sonia, I woke up this morning feeling the full anticipation of my Heart's Desire just waiting to happen. Yet I knew as I thought about it that I had to have tremendous faith to keep myself on track. With this in mind, I got in my car to come to my appointment with you, and as I pulled up to a red light, I found myself right behind a car whose license plate read 'LP O'FTH'!

"Smiling to myself over this coincidence, I continued to make my way across the city to your office and found myself stuck behind the *slowest* taxi in Chicago! It was driving me crazy. After many failed attempts to pass him, I just gave up. Finally I did have a chance to pull alongside him at a red light and saw he had a sign in the window that read

Faith brings down before our eyes
the strongest walls.
Faith makes us victorious
and helps us win the battles.

"This second message really hit me. No doubt about it, God really was telling me to relax and have faith!" she said, laughing. "It's funny—just seeing those two signs gives me the patience and faith I need."

Sally is on the threshold of her dream, and her faith will see it through.

FORGIVENESS LIGHTENS THE LOAD

The surest way to find the faith required at this point is to forgive anybody and everybody (including yourself) who may have hurt you or let you down in the past. Sometimes our unwillingness to forgive is a way to protect ourselves from further hurts, but it really attaches us all the more firmly to our pain. And as long as we direct our anger toward those who have victimized or hurt us, they still hold our attention and our power. Even our greatest oppressors cannot keep us down as long as we own our power of forgiveness.

Last year, fifty years after my mother's release from a concentration camp, my older sister and I took her and my father back to Germany to revisit the scene of the crime.

Not knowing exactly how she would respond to awakening such long-ago and painful memories, I could feel my protective instincts running high. I was afraid that her memories might prove to be overwhelming, and part of me worried the trip would open a Pandora's box, although I had no reason to fear. My mother is spiritual person with an extraordinary point of view, and this trip was no exception.

When we first arrived in Germany and were loading our bags into our rental car at the airport, my mother spotted an armed soldier standing at the airport entrance. Looking at him, she said to us, "It seems odd to be standing here and not have to be afraid." The soldier, noticing her watching him as she talked, smiled at us. She smiled back.

As we drove along through the countryside I could see conflicting feelings move across her face. Sometimes she would point out a remembered spot but trail off when it came to giving us details. Sometimes she would reveal bits of a horrible scene she had endured, although never elaborating on anything painful for too long.

She told us how she was marched on foot by Nazi soldiers for fourteen days with barely any food or water and of course no protection from the elements. She told us how the soldiers shaved the prisoners' heads and burned their clothes and threw everyone into tents without any facilities or heat. She revealed these vignettes in increments, mostly thinking out loud.

At one point she told us how the soldier lined up prisoners and then gunned them down right before her horrified twelve-year-old eyes. They then threw bags of lime over the bodies to cover them up, only to do it again with more prisoners. She frequently lapsed into silence, and I could tell she was in deep contemplation of what had happened so many years ago. I could hardly believe that my mother, who was so loving and optimistic, had undergone so much pain and terror.

Much to my surprise, as we approached the town where my mothers had been released, she said spontaneously, "Look how beautiful this countryside has become. Even the darkest ignorance can't prevent the beauty of God from manifesting all around."

Later, when we went to the church where they had married after the liberation, my parents told us how my mother had worn a wedding gown made from a parachute. In spite of the fact that my father was a member of the occupying forces and my mother was a former prisoner, everyone put aside the hatreds of war for that one day and the whole town came to the church to celebrate their wedding. The townspeople somehow found an old horse and buggy, and one kind man even came up with an old silver saddle, which he polished to a brilliant shine and put on the horse to drive my surprised parents to their reception in style.

My mother and father stood hand in hand, at the foot of the church steps just as they had fifty years before. Musing over those long-ago days, she said, "It's amazing to be standing here again— free, with my family, and feeling so blessed." Then she shook her head in a melancholy way and said, "I forgive them all. They didn't know what they were doing."

Choose to view all old hurts as necessary steps along the way to your dream. Success is, after all, the outcome of those failures, and each missed mark does bring you closer to what you want.

Realize that you may be tired. Coming this far means that you have been working very hard and have earned a well-deserved rest. Trust that the Universe will continue to work its magic on your behalf even if you need to take a breather. So many people fear that if they rest their efforts at this point, they will thwart their progress toward a miracle. Yet easing up may be exactly what you must do now, in order for your miracle to occur. My teacher Dr. Tully once said, "Sonia, sometimes the most powerful thing you can do is nothing!"

Urgency is the voice of fear. So is contriving, coercion, and manipulation. Fear is the voice of the false self, the lesser ego mind trying to prevent you from remembering who you really are, a spiritual creative being. After all, once you do, the ego gets a demotion from its accustomed position as ruler of things, for it must step aside and allow Divine spirit to take over. Fear chokes off the flow of spirit and stops things altogether.

If you are fearful at this time, make a concerted effort to pray. It isn't necessary to beg, bargain, cajole, plead, or negotiate what you want in the way of prayer, however. In fact, please *don't* do that, because if you give in to your fears of unworthiness, you will actually be thrown backward. The best way to pray right now is to say

> *Divine spirit, release me from my fears*
> *and help me to remember who I am.*

If you find yourself in a crisis of faith—go outside! Observe nature. See the generosity of Divine spirit in the world around you. Walk among trees. Breathe in the oceans and lakes and streams. Drinks in the beauty of flowers. Listen for the music of birds. Notice the miracles abounding all around you.

If you have followed Principles One through Six, your prayers will transform your fears into calm anticipation of your miracle. Know that a loving Universe is happy to gift you with your dream. Know that you are as worthy of a miracle as anyone, but that the Universe is wiser than you in how to deliver it. Trust that God in his infinite vision knows better than you how to bring your dreams about.

One client of mine, Daniel, was struggling with Principle Number Seven. He was an actor who felt that the Universe was taking much too long to deliver his Heart's Desire: a steady acting career. In fact, he was angry about it. He followed all the rules, he applied his full energy to the creative Principles, he did everything right—yet his career limped along sporadically, and he was forced to wait on tables to pay the bills.

"When is it my turn?" he asked for the fifth year in a row at his annual reading. "I feel like this is just another rerun of last years' saga."

"Not yet," I said. "Give it a few more years."

"I'll be an old man by then," he joked. "I'll be doing dinner theater in the retirement home." Frustrated but making light of it, he went back to the restaurant, still struggling along.

One day he called me, out of breath. "Sonia, I just had the most wonderful surprise! On a recent trip to London, I went on a casting call recommended by my agent. I can't believe it yet, but they cast me in a major play—as an aging waiter!" He was preparing to move there within the week to begin rehearsals.

"Isn't that the wildest?" he finished.

"I think it's Divine humor," I said.

It was his first big break after years of trying. The Universe was always on the job, and the alchemy of God converged all the elements into an ideal career launch. It's been three years since then, and he's been steadily acting ever since. In his case, both aging and working as a waiter were the necessary steps to achieving his dream.

THE UNIVERSE IS READY WHEN YOU ARE

Gino, a favorite client of mine, was an inner-city cop who was deeply devoted to spiritual growth. He read metaphysical books voraciously, attended every self-improvement seminar he could find, meditated, went on spiritual quests, and had even walked on fire. Gino was very knowledgeable about the Principles of Creativity.

His Heart's Desire was to make a difference to the world, and particularly with his police department. Having put in twenty years on the force, he was intimately familiar with problems of police abuse. He felt that most of these problems involved officers who were not conscious of their true soul essence and were working out of fear and greatly inflated egos.

Gino wanted to devise a plan to teach officers how to face their fears through meditation, physical endurance tests, and instruction about the soul. He worked long and hard over his plans until he had perfected a training program designed specifically for police officers' needs, to help them break through their fears and work from the authentic power of love. Gino was absolutely certain, deep in his bones, that this training program was his life's purpose.

Too bad no one else thought so. Gino tried to engage the support of his superiors, with no luck. He met with the mayor's office and was sent away. He revised his idea over and over again, making it more and more financially feasible. No dice.

He prayed. He meditated. He imagined. He prepared. He loved. But no one else cared. He was completely unsuccessful.

Gino pursued his dream for two years, with enthusiasm, and didn't progress even one inch. Finally, disillusioned, he gave up.

"Screw this!" he said. "I'm offering my service and no one wants it."

Worn-out and emotionally bankrupt, Gino threw in the towel and walked away. Confused over his rejection, he decided to develop new interests. He bought a motorcycle and a house and started to take pleasure in focusing on himself. Eventually his frustration lessened. He enjoyed fixing up his house, and riding his motorcycle gave him a sense of freedom and possibility. He made new friends, ones he wasn't interested in saving.

With all these changes he began to feel a real sense of peace of mind and anonymity. As he put it, "I'm codependent no more!"

Imagine Gino's surprise when, more than two years after his first proposed his training program, he received a call from the mayor's office. They were now very much interested in pursuing his ideas, and they wanted to meet with him about his course proposal!

He was ecstatic.

In retrospect, Gino realized that even though he wanted to teach his fellow officers to move past their egos, at the time he proposed his idea he still had a whole lot of ego left himself. Indeed, he was out to "save the police force" single-handedly and really thought he could. The two-year waiting period had taught him to surrender his ego and become more connected to simply nurturing himself and his life. Now he really was in a position to teach from an honestly loving perspective and not from a need to rescue anyone.

Principle Number Seven was diligently working through Gino all along. It is the Principle of surrendering any and all attachment to the outcome. It means letting go and allowing the Universe to do the magic in its own way and knowing that the Universe's magic is always better than your own. Principle Number Seven teaches that the Universe has its own timing and its own vision. Just as every growing season requires the passage of a certain amount of time, so it is with our creative dreams—they too need time to evolve in "season." Realize that your personal vision is limited and turn your power over to a higher view.

Principle Number Seven is the Principle of patience, a very difficult lesson in a world motivated by instant gratification. It is the teacher of time. It asks that you move your consciousness out of your head, where you want things to go your way *now*, and into your heart, where you want things to go your way *now*, and into your heart, where you begin to go with the Universal flow of God. It asks that you shift your awareness into your heart, the seat of your soul, where you can feel that all is well in a deep intuitive way, and wait patiently for Providence.

If impatience and lack of faith are regular problems for you, try saying this prayer that my mother taught me as a child:

Divine spirit, use me. Take me to my purpose.

Then relax and take a break. Know your dream is quietly being worked on behind the scenes even if you can't see it or control it. That is when you move from knowledge and into wisdom.

Patience and faith are the two greatest tests of the human soul.

It is so much easier to go by what our give physical sense convey. It is easier to trust when we can see, hear, touch, smell, and taste the reality of our desires.

We all struggle like Doubting Thomases from time to time. But does that mean that what our senses tell us is all that exists? Hardly—especially considering that the information your sense convey is very inaccurate most of the time. Better to use your insight than your eyesight. Better to listen to your intuition than to others, present or past. Better to tune in to the deeper, more profound levels of energy than to simply take in the surface appearance of things.

Principles Number Seven asks you to have faith, but that doesn't mean blind, naïve faith. It means the faith of a fully awakened perspective. Tune your awareness in to the flow of your creativity and feel God working through you in unseen, even mysterious ways. Quiet your mind with meditation and prayer. Center your awareness on your heart. Allow yourself the luxury and generosity of knowing that Divine spirit is lovingly working on your behalf. Even if you are at rest, the engines of creative motion are working diligently behind the scenes.

If you are put through a test of patience, accept it gracefully. Take it as an indication that you are getting very close to your Heart's Desire. I can guarantee you that the wait is worth it. At the right moment the dominoes will fall into place as lightly as feathers, as if by magic—universal magic.

Principle Number Seven is true power. With faith and patience you align the creative forces exactly, so that your dream unfolds through no effort or force. This is called creative surrender—complete creative surrender.

What you are surrendering is all illusion that keeps your dream from coming through, all illusion that you cannot have what you want. You surrender the illusion that you must fight for what you want, that it must be painful and dramatic, that there are forces preventing you from realizing your dream, or that you will fail. What you are surrendering is a "me against the world" perspective, the perspective that looks through the viewfinder of your ego, your false self, and keeps you frightened and insecure.

When you surrender, you remember that you are a Divine soul, inseparable from God, guided by God. You also see the absolute connection you have to all God's grace and good, like rays that are connected to the sun. What you see is your true worth as a child of the Universe, infinitely loved and supported.

YOU'RE THE CHANNEL, NOT THE SOURCE

In my Heart's Desire workshop I illustrate what having faith means by placing a standing lamp in the center of the room. Trying to operate out of personal will is like trying to light the bulb without plugging into an electrical source. First of all, you won't succeed. Second, you'll exhaust yourself trying. And third, in reality it's ridiculous not to realize that plugging in the lamp is the only way to light the bulb!

We are no different from that lamp. We too are supported by a Higher Source than ourselves. This Universal energy flowing through us is the source of our life and breath. This energy gives us the ability to create. This Universal source of life force is Divine spirit.

When we remember that we are a part of Divine spirit made manifest, and that Universal energy is infinitely at our disposal through simply "plugging in" to faith, then we can begin to understand how we *already* have all the power in the Universe available to us, simply by allowing it to flow. We don't have to manipulate this force, just allow it.

The reason people struggle with faith is that we have forgotten that we are souls. We have become disconnected from the truth of our existence. When we forget our spiritual nature and become manipulated by our own egos, we become afraid, consumed by anxiety and insecurity, because the ego is not our true self and cannot live on its own power.

Coming back to the truth of who you really are is central to Principle Number Seven. Once you do, fear ceases to rule you and trust settles in. Faith comes as easily as breathing if you search for it through the eyes of your soul. In fact, it comes without even a pause.

Patience is the front door to faith. If you come to this door, know that you, your dream, and the Universe are still moving into alignment but aren't quite there yet. Be excited when you arrive at this point! It means that you are doing your part as you should, and your miracle is on the way to being born.

Principle Number Seven tells us that there is more work to be done, but the work remaining should be executed in calm, quiet trust that your dream is well on its way. It reminds you that a much greater power than your own, a behind-the-scenes power of the Universe, is organizing everything into perfect order on your behalf.

Now let's move on to practicing Principle Number Seven.

PRACTICING THE SEVENTH PRINCIPLE

Creating an alchemy box

Your dreams and desires are sacred and holy because they arise from your most authentic self, your soul. As with any act of faith, as practiced by all religions worldwide since the beginning of time, what is called for here is a ritual to illustrate your soul's commitment to your dream.

The ritual that best encompasses all that you have been working on, and your agreement to surrender your personal will into the hands of god now, is one that I was given by a shaman and teacher friends, LuAnn Glatzmaier. She showed me how to create an alchemy box. Alchemy means transformation, and this box will transform your energy into reality.

Making an alchemy box is great fun and stimulates all your creative energy while you work. The process takes time and preparation, each act being a decision from you to support your Heart's Desire in a most outwardly kinesthetic way. Don't worry about not having the time. Every step is manageable. The entire activity can be accomplished by spending ten to fifteen minutes a day for a week.

Let me show you how.

Phase One

First you will need a box with a lid or a closeable cover. Good choices are a shoebox, a cookie tin, or a hatbox. You may also find a suitable box in a mail packaging and shipping center. What won't work well is the kind of shirt box or flat gift box found in a department store. Look in your closets and cupboards. A suitable box may be waiting there for you.

Next you will need to begin collecting scissors, glue, sheets of beautiful tissue or origami paper, and things to decorate your box with, as well as things to put inside your box to create a magical energy. Keep your eyes open for special items that represent your dream. You may find that they will simply pop up in your path. For example, you may receive a postcard or see a photograph on a magazine cover at the grocery checkout line that perfectly represents your dream.

Once you commit to creating your box, the Universe will join in enthusiastically to offer you ideas and materials. This phase of the project is like a treasure hunt, and you will be directed by your soul and your spirit guides to many marvelous things. Allow at least a week to collect your materials. That way you will have a full seven-day magical experience.

Save all of your articles in a special place as you collect them. Some things you may collect for your box are

- holy pictures (angels, saints, Buddha, menorahs, Stars of David...)
- pictures of celestial beings (angels, fairies, earth spirits...)
- pictures of animals (birds, lions, horses, dogs, wild deer...)
- photos of landscapes that represent places you want to visit
- photos of people who look like the ones you'd like to meet
- images of creative media you'd like to use (such as paintbrushes, cameras, typewriters, garden tools, musical instruments...)
- pictures of people working in areas you would like to work in

You can cut pictures out of magazines. You can find images on gift cards. You can photocopy images from tarot decks—or better yet, you can even draw your own.

Another wonderful source for decorating your alchemy box is your local kids' store or card shop where stickers are sold. There are literally hundreds you can choose from that are beautiful and representative of the experience you are invoking, such as

hearts	angels
houses	fairies
dollar signs	starbursts
musical instruments	flowers
caps and gowns	animals

You can decorate your entire box, outside and inside, simply by using stickers. You can make a collage of words and glue it across your box. You can glue on rhinestones, plastic jewels, feathers, and colored tissue paper.

You can find a photo of yourself in your happiest moment and glue it to the inside cover of your box. You may also want to glue a small pocket mirror to the inside cover to reflect who you are and what your heart longs for.

An arts and crafts store can be marvelous source of materials. There you can find colorful glitter glues, brightly colored tapes, sprinkles, sparkles, and confetti that you can glue on or sprinkle inside your box. You can also get pages of alphabet and number stickers to create your own stick-on messages.

But decorating your box needn't be limited to covering its surfaces. You can also put things into your box to further energize its magic, such as

- dried lavender and roses (for calming and love)
- dried cedar (for grounding and support)
- religious and metaphysical talismans (for spiritual inspiration, such as rosaries, angel pins, tiny images of Buddha, pictures of Christ, menorahs, Stars of David, images of animals)
- replicas of your desires (toy babies, houses, money, hearts)
- incense to sweeten and invoke a sense of the Divine or holy (frankincense, copal, myrrh, benzoin)

Here are some ideas my students have come up with:

- money, fake or real, if you want prosperity
- a little plastic baby if you want a child
- toy cars if you want a new car
- miniencyclopedias if you want to go back to school
- tiny wedding cake bride and groom if you want to get married
- miniature photos of the sun if you want health and life force

Phase Two

In phase two you actually put together your alchemy box. This usually takes an uninterrupted block of two to three hours. It's an excellent alternative to TV or talking on the phone and is exquisitely empowering, so it should be planned well in advance.

During this phase, take your time and don't begin until you are ready. There is value in creating a degree of anticipation as you prepare for the work.

It is very helpful to play music that soothes you as you work on your box, and be certain to shut off the TV, unplug the phone, and do anything else that will allow you to be completely undistracted.

Assemble all of your materials before you start decorating the box itself. An excellent and beautiful way to cover the box is to use colored tissue paper and decoupage glue. You can choose whatever colors you want, and the glue brushes on like paint. Another way to cover your box is to use pictures of your Heart's Desire from magazines or books and glue them all over the inside and outside of your box.

Once you have decorated the box itself, you will want to fill it with your magical talismans and earth elements. This is the time to put in your lavender, roses, cedar chips, incense, and any other special items. (Inside my own box I have a crystal bluebird of happiness, coins from Egypt, pebbles from India, crystals from Sedona, red feathers for power, a white candle for inspiration, a Hershey's Kiss for sweetness, a tarot card of the Fool for surprise, and a Monopoly house for safe dwelling, just to name a few items.)

Let the child in you come out and play while doing this project. Count on your own imagination to deliver appropriate and inspirational images to you. Synchronicity will surely play a part in all of this, and what you need will pop into your mind.

Let this entire activity be a three-dimensional symbolic representation of what your soul is working to create in your life. Notice your emotions as you work on your dream. Feel yourself empowering your dream.

The making of your alchemy box is a synthesis of all that you have been working on in Principles One through Seven. It embodies focus, belief, imagination, commitment, intuition, and love. It will come together with enthusiasm and create a safe magical haven for your dreams. Let phase two soothe your soul, engage your creative spirit, and celebrate your dreams as they move toward manifestation.

Phase Three

After you have created a beautiful alchemy box to receive your innermost dreams, you are ready for phase three. You will need a sheet or two of beautiful paper, such as Japanese origami paper, and a pair of scissors. Start by cutting your sheet of paper into you four pieces. On each piece of paper write down what your heart desires. You can write as many desires as you are willing to be responsible for.

Then, one at a time, place each Heart's Desire into the box, saying this prayer:

> *Divine Father, Divine Mother*
> *I surrender my dream into*
> *your sacred hands, and confidently await*
> *your generous deliverance.*

Then place your dreams into your sacred vessel, close the lid, and hide it in a safe place where it will be undisturbed.

Some students and clients have told me that even though they love the idea of making an alchemy box, they find it difficult to motivate themselves to actually do the work. This is understandable in a world where creativity and playfulness are viewed as "silly" and "wasteful." If you find your creativity is blocked when you try to make your sacred box, ask a friend, your kids, or neighbors to join you in the project and work together. Anything shared with another enthusiastic person takes on far greater appeal. You'd be surprised how willing others will be to join you if you let them in on the magic of it all.

If this doesn't appeal to you, then you can simply choose to find or buy a beautiful box that's already made. You may even have one right on the shelf at home. Look around. It can be a cookie tin, a hat box, a cigar box, a jewelry box, or simply a cardboard box. If you can't find a suitable box at home, then go shopping for one. They are everywhere—and very beautiful at that. And for those who will even fail to do this, here is my last suggestion: Decorate a large envelope and use this as your sacred vessel. Even this will work for you. After all, it's not the box (or envelope) that is magical, but your intended use of it that makes it special.

Releasing the playfulness in you is a very powerful component to creating your dreams, but it's okay to play in a way that is comfortable for you. Handmade, hand-selected, and handwritten are all personal choices, and are equally valid, as long as you make the choice to manifest the sacred vessel you need to surrender your dreams into the loving hands of the Universe.

MEDITATION

Sit comfortably in a chair with your back straight and your feet flat on the ground. Close your eyes and allow your breathing to fall into a smooth, natural rhythm.

> *Imagine that the bottoms of your feet are turning into roots, traveling deep into the ground. Imagine with each breath you exhale that you are becoming a beautiful, strong tree.*
> *As you inhale, imagine yourself deeply rooted to the earth. See yourself solidly supported by the earth's loving energy.*

Imagine drawing the earth's energy up through your body, starting with your feet and traveling through your legs and trunk, flowing through your arms to your heart, and continuing to the top of your head and out into the limitless Universe.

As you exhale, imagine all personal anxieties and efforts draining out of your body through the roots and flowing into the earth. With each breath you inhale, feel the limitless support available to you.

Make no effort to support yourself through your personal will. Know that you are part of the Divine scheme of things and that you and your dream are lovingly being cared for.

Relax with a few more breaths, and then, when you are ready, slowly open your eyes.

REVIEW

When you have completed your alchemy box ritual, peacefully move on to Principle Number Eight. If you haven't been able to complete it, return to Principles Six and Seven and review them.

PRINCIPLE NUMBER EIGHT

Claim Your Dream

As you progress from Principle to Principle you begin to understand that the process of creative manifestation is very logical. By following each Principle, you move step by step along the path, ushering your desires into your life. The veil of sentimentality you may have worn begins to lift as you realize that you all your desires can be fulfilled if you meet certain conditions for Divine energy to flow through you.

In Principles One, Two, and Three you realize that identifying your Heart's Desire is the essential beginning and that you can best manifest what is born from your heart, not from fear. You also realize that desire alone will not bring about fulfillment.

Principles Four, Five and Six teach that mere desire, without clarity, organization, and steady effort, will remain dormant. As you work through these principles you begin to shape your desire into an energized intention, accumulating power and force as you go.

The first three Principles create on the emotional plane. The second three create on the mental plane. And the last three concentrate on finally releasing this energy into the physical plane, where you can enjoy your creation.

Each goal, each desire, follows a creative life path very similar to your own physical evolution. Like you, each dream starts out as a seed idea, initially possessing the full potential of expression in unmanifested form. Like you, each dream starts out as a seed idea, initially possessing the full potential of expression in unmanifested form. Like you, each desire begins to organize energy, taking on shape, form, and size. When this shape evolves sufficiently, it establishes its intention to stay, as you once did. And once committed to, each dream develops a heartbeat of its own, compelling your choices and actions to support it. Each creation intrinsically follows its own evolution and its own timing and will fail or die if forced into being before it is really ready to be born.

Eventually, however, the time arrives for your dream to express itself into the world, to begin to assert itself on the physical plane, and the vehicle that carries your dream from mental to physical expression can be found, literally, right under your nose. Principle Number Eight is stated simply and elegantly in Genesis: "In the beginning was the Word."

This Principle announces your greatest power of all, the power to create exactly what you want by *speaking* it into creation. God created the Universe with words: "Let there be light." Jesus worked miracles with words: "Say the word and you are healed." Moses was given the power of God in words—the Ten Commandments—to lead his people from slavery to freedom.

Words create everything, because words are the embodiment of thought. They announce all that you focus on, all that you believe. They define your inner landscape and reveal your degree of commitment. Words reveal your beliefs and express your enthusiasm. Words come from fear or from faith. They are the summary of your creative efforts in motion, the energetic substance that channels Universal spirit and forms your physical experience.

The words you choose are programmed to release power and life force into whatever they express. As you speak, so you experience—whether you want to or not. Your words are the full transference of your energy from psychic to physical expression.

They are indeed the magic wand of creativity.

Unfortunately you are probably unconscious of this power and so aren't careful about what you create. The truth is that whether or not you know it, whether or not you believe it or accept it, you are a Divine spiritual being and as such are the creator of your experience on earth. You may not be an effective creator because you haven't learned to align your life force with your desires—but *create?* You most certainly have!

Principle Number Eight asks you to fully own your Divine creative power and to take complete charge of how you use it. When you own your words, you assume your true identity as a being of light, made in the image and likeness of God. This Principle reveals the literal truth that Jesus taught when he said, "Don't you know that you are gods?"

Principle Number Eight is the secret to correcting all your mistakes. It instantly reveals the way to align your energy, creating a clear, unobstructed expression of your truth, your desires, on earth.

If your words, like seeds, are carelessly strewn about in aimless directions, then the energy embodied in these words will be weak, die off, and never grown into your dreams. If, however, you carefully, lovingly choose your words to specifically create the full intention of your dream, they will manifest your desire right before your astonished eyes—especially if those words are spoken with focus, intention, commitment, and love.

In other words—your word is law.

My mother was the first to reveal to me the creative power of words. She taught me that God gave us an incredible power to create whatever we wanted through our own words. If we put all of our energy behind our words, without any doubt, then what we said would come true. The secret was to speak *without any doubt.*

This idea was fascinating, and it opened up a whole new world of possibility for me. If I could learn the Principles, I could create anything! I experimented with the Principle over and over. Then, at age thirteen, I got what I considered positive proof.

I was watching TV one day during Christmas season, and I saw that one of the local stations was doing a promotion. Santa Claus was driving around Denver, looking for anyone who put the words "KWGN Merry Christmas Santa" on a big sign in their window. If you put up a sign it was spotted by the TV Santa, he would stop in and give you a giant color TV.

To a thirteen-year-old in a family that didn't have much money, the idea of winning a large color TV sounded fantastic. I decided to use my full energy and the power of my word to get that TV. I wrote down "KWGN Merry Christmas Santa. Love, Sonia" on a big sign and said out loud, with my full energy, "Santa, come to my house *now*" as I taped it to our window.

I was really excited because I had absolutely no doubt that Santa would come. It was a very powerful sensation. My brothers and sisters watched me, amused.

"Do you think you'll win?" my sister Noelle asked as I put on the tape.

"Mark my words," I said (an expression my mother used all the time), "that TV is mine. Santa will come!"

That happened on Thursday night. Friday after school I came home to find my mother very excited.

"You'll never guess what happened today," she said, smiling.

"What, what?" I cried.

"At seven forty-five, two minutes after you left for school, when I was still in my nightgown with no makeup on, the doorbell rang. When I opened the door a TV camera was in my face, with Santa Claus right behind it, handing me a brand-new TV! I just about died of embarrassment. So waiting for you in the living room is your new color TV from Santa, Sonia, and I'll be on the evening news in my underwear!"

We all squealed with delight. Less than twenty-four hours after I had used the power of the word, the TV arrived from Santa.

That was my Christmas miracle and a life-changing experience. The reward of a new TV was enough evidence for me to begin believing in the power of words. I soon realized, however, that there are two sides to every coin.

I remember that on one occasion when I was a teenager, full swing into my rebellious period, I wanted to wander around downtown with my friends one Friday night, but my mother said no. It made me angry, so I decided to lie and say I was baby-sitting to get out of the house. I knew I was ignoring Principle Number Eight as well as my mom, but I thought I could get away with it.

I met my girlfriends at the corner and we sneaked downtown. Our big thrill for the night was riding up and down the elevators at the Hilton Hotel. (Don't ask me why—we were teenagers!) All the while I kept talking to my girlfriends about how I had lied, how uncomfortable I felt about it, and how awful it would be if I got caught.

Because my worries were ruining the fun, my girlfriends eventually started teasing me about it. Soon my compromised position became the butt of so many silly jokes that even I began to join in. We made up ridiculous scenarios of me getting caught by my mom in the elevator, and then we burst into hysterical laughter.

Throughout my friends assured me, "Don't worry! Your mom *never* comes here, Sonia. You're just being paranoid."

They had no more said this than we arrived in the lobby once again and the elevator doors opened. Standing there face-to-face with me, waiting for the elevator, was...

"Oh, my God! No!"

...my mom.

We all screamed with surprise. My girlfriend Sue made a desperate attempt to hide me by pushing the close button on the elevator, but it was too late. My mom, as shocked to see me as I was to see her, reached out to grab me. To really sink my boat, the doors came closing in on her, which only irritated her more.

I was doomed. I could hear "taps" playing in my head.

"I gotta go, guys," I said as I stepped out of the elevator and walked toward my funeral.

After I got the lecture only an angry psychic mother could give, I mustered up the courage to ask, "By the way, Mom, why *were* you at the Hilton, anyway?"

She said, "My spirits told me to go!"

To myself I thought, "Your *spirits* didn't tell you to go—*I* did, by blabbering for two hours with my big mouth about getting caught." It was Principle Number Eight in action.

That night I learned about the creative power of words. Never say what you don't want to experience. (And never try to outsmart a psychic mother.)

That experience made a huge impression on me. From that night on I began to notice the connection between what people said and what they experienced, only to discover again and again just how consistent this Principle was. If I'd had any doubts about this Principle in the beginning, over the years the doubts have completely disappeared.

What I have observed is that Principle Number Eight is the most easily verifiable Principle of all. The truth is that we are like gods and goddesses who talk in our sleep, using the power of our own words quite unconsciously and most of the time against ourselves. I guess the ancient Chinese knew the literal power of creative words when they said, "Be careful what you ask for. You may get it." I realize there is no "maybe" about it. You *do* get it. It's the law.

For example, I have watched people create absolute nightmares of experience using the power of the word. They elaborate on what they don't want. They describe the worst. They lament disappointment and disaster. They are wishy-washy and dishonest.

They repeat what others say instead of listening to their Higher Selves. They enthusiastically complain, languish in fear, and sing the blues. And in keeping with Principle Eight, one by one they manifest perfectly—a perfectly awful experience.

My client Lois, an art teacher who worked in a crowded public school, came to me for a reading because she was not supported by the school principal, who saw little importance in her work. The struggle between them wore Lois out, and eventually she hated getting up and going to school.

During our conversation she said no fewer than ten times, "I truly dislike the principal of the school. He is such a pain in the neck."

I also found out that Lois suffered chronic neck and shoulder pain and was on disability leave.

Tom, a newly hired ad agent, came for a reading because his job was very competitive and he worried constantly about losing his position. He didn't have the temperament to be as aggressive as his company demanded.

"I can't stomach the competition," Tom told me while eating Rolaids. He suffered from a chronic ulcer and bouts of intestinal trauma.

Nadine, a mother of six, had devoted her entire life to raising her children. She came to me for a reading as her last child was moving from Kansas to the East Coast.

"It breaks my heart to see the last one go," she said with a sigh, "but I'm happy for her."

Four months later Nadine had a heart attack.

In following the law, all three of these clients suffered the literal translation of their own words. Words are the foot soldiers of your power and will execute your orders exactly as you give them.

In Principle Number Two you learned that your subconscious mind creates what you dwell on. In Principle Number Eight you reveal to the world what you are focusing on and command the Universe to create it for you. Divine spirit in its infinite love has endowed you with the ability and the freedom to create whatever you choose, good or bad. It doesn't matter. Creation begins with thoughts and ends with words, and the process holds true *no matter what the goal.*

The amazing part is that in reality, creating illness, disappointment, and poverty takes much more effort than creating success. It's very draining to concentrate on doom and gloom. Imagining misery is intense emotional work. Reiterating old memories of pain and injury requires meticulous efforts of reconstruction. Ignoring your intuition sets up a struggle. Working with resentment or anger is exhausting, and living in fear is almost unbearable.

Speaking with this kind of intensely negative energy will make you sick. When you channel words from this intensely negative frame of consciousness, it is the equivalent of dropping a bomb on your Heart's Desire and blowing it to bits.

Realize that it's much easier to direct that energy into what you *love.* Even if you use only half the energy you have put toward conjuring up problems, you are bound to succeed because love amplifies your efforts.

They beauty of the Principles of Creativity is that they can work both forward and backward simultaneously. Say what you want. Claim it out loud to the Universe. Whistle it while you work. Shout it from the highest mountain. Quietly meditate on it in your prayers. Call it your own.

A client once told me a story about owning her dream. She said that she went to a prosperity workshop where the instructor stood in front of the room and held up a dollar bill.

"This bill," she said, "is for all the people in this room who have their bills paid."

About eight people raised their hands. The instructor gave them each a dollar. Next she held up a five-dollar bill.

"This bill," she said, "is for all the people in this room who have their bills paid."

About eight people raised their hands. The instructor gave them each a dollar. Next she held up a five-dollar bill.

"This five-dollar bill is for all those here who have their bills paid *and* savings in the bank."

This time only five people raised their hands. She gave each of them five dollars.

Next she held up a hundred-dollar bill and said, "This hundred is for the person in the room with a very special qualification. Only I am not going to say what that qualification is. You must figure that out for yourself. The person who does can have it."

The room fell silent as everyone tried to figure out what the special qualification could be. They looked to the left and right at each other, hoping for a clue.

Finally a woman jumped up and said, "I have it! That hundred-dollar bill is mine!" And she walked right up and took the bill from the smiling instructor. Surprised, everyone looked to the instructor for an explanation.

The instructor said to the woman, "Would you like to tell the rest of the group what your special qualification is?"

The woman answered, "The courage to claim it for myself!"

This is a clear example of someone owning her dream. Can you own yours? When you can, it becomes as available to you as the hundred-dollar bill was to that woman. All it took for her to get the money was to say "It's mine!" and reach out to claim it.

Sounds simple, yet so few people dare to claim what could so easily be theirs. Those who do have moved energy right into their own hands. This energy is called *conviction*.

In my metaphysical studies of the cabala and the tree of life, I learned that words spoken with conviction form actual magnets and attract back to the speaker, measure for measure, exactly what was broadcast into the world. When you speak with conviction and confidence you amplify this magnetizing force a thousandfold.

Conviction calls your desires home. Confidence guides them directly to you. Ownership through your words places your desires in your hands. Words spoken with conviction convey your Divine power. And "if God is with you, who is against you? There is no greater power than God."

"I AM" IS LAW

The two most powerful words in our lexicon are "I am." The ancient Hebrew name for God, Yahweh, translates literally as "I am that I am." Creating in the name of God by using "I am" commands the entire Universe to obey. When you say "I am," you add a powerful punch to your words, and you can be certain that what you claim *will* come to be. That's why you should never proclaim your limitations unless you're prepared to own them—the words "I am" are the most powerful words of ownership in the Universe.

Knowing this can release all of your potential and manifest it into material form. My teacher Charlie Goodman taught me a wonderful way to manifest through the words "I am."

Whatever you desire, pretend you already own it. I follow his instructions and seized upon those words, pretending "I am psychic." And twenty-five years later I can tell you truthfully that I *am* psychic. Use your power to own your truth. Claim out loud who you are. Remember your Divine truth. Open your heart and release, for all the world to hear, "I am who I am."

"I am an artist."

"I am loved."

"I am prosperous."

"I am beautiful."

"I am secure."

"I am creative."

"I am worthy just as I am."

WHEN YOU SAY "I AM," IT'S TRUE

Did you know that the Universe will not let you be anything less than the god or goddess that you are, and as such, it completely respects your power to create? It's true, and sometimes this can be a little awkward.

Have you ever had your words come back to haunt you? Have you ever been caught in little white lies? Or worse? Probably so, because if lies are to be believed, they must be spoken with conviction—and as you are learning, words spoken with conviction *create*.

The Universe does not make a distinction between truth and lies. Every word is simply a creative command released and magnetized, programmed to attract its complementary physical form to you. I learned this as a teenager when I got caught in the elevator by my mother. And you can see it around you every day.

My friend once told me that she called her old hairdresser while sitting in her new hairdresser's chair, to ask for the formula for her hair color. Not wanting to tell the truth about where she was, she lied and said she was calling from out of town. Two hours later, walking to her car with freshly colored hair, she ran into her old hairdresser, face-to-face.

Several months ago my neighbor called in to work sick because she wanted a few days off to relax. She told her supervisor she had the flu and was bedridden. Later that day she ate a bad tunafish sandwich and got a case of food poisoning that forced her to stay in bed for two days.

A client told me that she was once dating two men at the same time. One day at the last minute she broke a date with one of the men in order to accept a spontaneous dinner invitation from the other. The lie she told to break the date was that she was delayed at work. But no sooner had she gotten out of the car with the second man in front of the restaurant than the first man pulled into a parking space behind them and headed into the same restaurant with his mother.

Embarrassing? Yes, but nevertheless her own creation! The Universe honors your Divinity by honoring your words. So own what you say—because you *will* own it anyway.

Principle Number Eight is the Principle of accountability. It brings home the reality that no matter what you want, you must be prepared to own it, to take care of it, to be responsible for it, to call it your own.

Your words reveal whether or not this is so. If you pray for one thing but say another in your everyday encounters, ask yourself whether you are revealing an inner reluctance to be in charge of your dream.

My client Millie was forty-three years old. She was very eclectic and had a hand in a million different projects. She painted, she worked as a member of a charitable organization, she gardened, she traveled, she worked for a legal defense firm, she took part-time acting classes.

Millie loved her life, except for one bit problem. She had never been married, and she wanted to be. She dated constantly, but no proposals were forthcoming. She wanted to know when I saw a "prince" coming into her life.

"Never," I said. "I see opportunities, but not from princes."

Stunned by my answer, she said, "What an awful thing to say, Sonia. How on earth can you be so sure? You mean I'll *never* marry?"

"No," I said. "I mean there's no prince. Of course, I do see a few frogs who are interested in you but no princes."

"What do you mean?" she asked tearfully.

"I mean I see two men who are very eager to date you and perhaps marry you, but these men are not princes. They are frogs, who do frog-like things."

"Such as?"

"Well, they're only human. They forget important things, they're late, they don't have the thick black hair and muscular biceps you fantasize about. In fact, the men I see are a little overweight and thinning on top. But they are intensely interested in you, and they seem very sweet... Want to know about them?"

Millie, with her mouth open, looked appalled. "Good heavens, no. Why would I waste my time on men like that?"

"Well, Millie, 'that' is the male sex. All humans are frogs— they're flawed. All men have wonderful qualities, if you have the eyes to see. It's your ability to perceive their specialness that brings out their royal qualities. Of course," I added, smiling, "it takes patience and effort and a lot of love to build trust, but it does pay off."

She cringed. "I'm not sure I have the time or energy for that, especially if a man doesn't really excite me."

"That's why I'm telling you these things. What I observe is that you really don't want to be *married* at all, and what you do want, you have already."

"How so?" she asked.

'Those men you date now are princes, because any man can be a prince for an evening. It's just on a daily basis, that it's impossible, because it isn't natural to be in soft focus and slow motion every day. Life doesn't allow it."

She laughed. "Well, when you put it like that, I guess you're right. Maybe I'm asking for the worst possible thing. Maybe I should reconsider. After all, I really do enjoy my life, and I don't need to get into a situation with even more demands on my time. It's too precious."

"So forget about marriage, and enjoy your royal outings."

A year later Millie dropped me a lovely card that said she had indeed found her prince. He was a pilot who lived in his own apartment. He was in town three days a week, during which time they had fantastic fun together. Then he left for four days and she was alone to freely enjoy all her other interests. They were supremely happy, with no marriage plans.

Millie asked for a prince, and that's what she got. There was no "husband" about it.

USE YOUR WORDS CONSERVATIVELY

The last point I want to make about Principle Number Eight is something I learned many years ago from Dr. Tully.

Dr. Tully taught me that behind every word flows energy. If you use your words to gossip or babble about what you are going to do before you do it, then you are siphoning off the energy needed to actually do the work. Your words become an energy leak.

This is usually the root of the problem for those people who just can't seem to get up and get going to work on their dream. A case in point was a client of mine named Denise.

Denise very much wanted to be a newscaster. She spent hours and hours every day talking about how much she wanted it. She didn't even discriminate about whom she talked to. Anybody who would listen was just fine. She told them everything–how she planned to go to school, planned to take video classes, planned to write her résumé and send it out to the local stations. She talked about whom she'd talked with and whom they talked to and what they said.

The problem was that for all her talking, Denise could never find the time or motivation to follow through and do something. In reality all she did about her dream was talk. When it came time to walk her talk, to do something, she had exhausted the well. She had no reserve left to draw from.

Her subconscious mind was tricked into thinking she had accomplished something by all this talking, so it didn't give her the motivation to do the work. What Denise needed to do was *shut up*, and that's what I suggested.

"No matter how much talking you do, Denise, it will never be a substitute for action. *Ever.* Be quiet, and move the energy into your feet."

Denise took my advice. When she did "shut up" she realized all her talking was a substitute for real commitment. She realized that her pride had kept her from competing in the real world, so she tried to bolster herself up by impressing everyone with her hypothetical world. The trouble was, she was only fooling herself.

Her shutting up also shut off her misdirected efforts. Eventually it became so hard not to talk that she was compelled to channel that accumulated force into action. She took her first video class and enrolled in a journalism course at the university.

"It's slow," she said, "but at least I'm finally on my way for real. From now on I'm keeping my mouth shut."

Dr. Tully often said, "Talk only about what you've done, not about what you will do." Too often we waste our words on telling the world all we know, giving our suggestions and opinions before we have thought things through. The only time to utter advice is when you have direct experience and not just intellectual information. You may not fully understand the information you gather until you put it into practice.

It's always tempting to the ego to use intellectual knowledge to tell someone else how to create, because it is a convenient distraction from the work of creating our own happiness. This kind of effort doesn't create a thing for others or for you and therefore doesn't show up on the physical plane.

This is a very smart rule. Use your words conservatively. Waste is waste, on every level. Don't waste the energy you need by spending your words on idle chatter or on coaching someone else. Keeping your mouth shut will eventually move the energy into your feet, where it can do some real good.

I have seen how words, when used consciously and with great intention, can channel the Divine spirit of God behind them and heal in an instant. Words like these are what create miracles. And words like these can come from you.

PRACTICING THE EIGHTH PRINCIPLE

DON'T BE SHY—SPEAK UP

Every day, ask the Universe, *aloud,* for exactly what you need—the more specific, the better.

MUM'S THE WORD

When talking to others about your dreams, as yourself whether they are truly supportive or whether they will rain on your parade. So many clients have complained about how gung ho they were for their dream until someone (usually very close to them) sabotaged it with his or her own negativity.

Decide to stop talking about what you are *going* to do—share only what you *have* done. Remember, there's power in secrecy. Keep your dreams protected by silence.

TALKING THE TALK

Watch your words! If you want love, don't say no one loves you. If you want a new job, don't say there's no work to be had. Stop defending your pain and disappointment with your words.

Say only things that support your dream. If negative speech is hard to turn into positive speech, then at least get to the place of *no* speech.

NOTHING BUT THE TRUTH

Be honest and speak the truth. Don't lie—not to others, not to yourself. Speak honestly. This means both to others and to yourself as the words flow through your mind. When you speak the truth without exception, what you say becomes true.

A POSITIVE WORD

Words have power. Notice the words around you, and stay away from people who habitually speak in foul, angry, discouraging, or careless language. If you are subjected to someone's negative words, mentally say, "Cancel, cancel," as the words come toward you. (This is best said mentally, as you do not want to provoke more negative or damaging words of attack.)

THE POWER IS IN YOUR HANDS

Finally, assume full responsibility for the power of your words:

> *If you want love, speak lovingly.*
> *If you want money, speak generously.*
> *If you want health, speak wholesomely.*
> *If you want opportunity, speak creatively.*

HONESTY AND INTEGRITY

You tell the world who you are by your words. Build your miracle with the best possible choice of words. Let your words reveal your true essence and creative spirit at all times. Let your words honor you by honoring your words.

LISTEN TO YOURSELF

Speak to your Heart's Desire clearly into a voice recorder. When you are finished, rewind the recording and listen to your own voice. Do you sound convincing? Do you speak with clarity? Do you believe in yourself?

Repeat this exercise until you do speak with conviction.

AFFIRMATION

Use this empowering affirmation starting with the words "I am."

I am a creator
And I create with my words.
I honor my words,
My words honor me.
As I speak,
So it shall be.

You can use this affirmation or, better yet, create an affirmation in your own words. Say it every time you are tempted to complain or recite your fears. Say it when you are discouraged. Say it when you are insecure. Say it when you wake up in the morning and just before you go to bed.

Make this affirmation a part of your daily routine.

REVIEW

If you have completed these exercises, move on to Principle Number Nine.

If you haven't, back up and review Principles Seven and Eight.

Stay True to Your Dream

As you approach the final step in manifesting your Heart's Desire, you now understand that success is not a random event, although it can be a spontaneous one. You begin to see that there is no luck involved, but there is the presence of grace. A dream doesn't just happen; rather, it is the direct result of your meeting certain conditions and laws so that you become an unobstructed channel of Divine expression.

Each Principle in this workbook establishes ever-increasing agreement between your creative desire and your conscious and unconscious intentions. Each Principle we have practiced reminds you of who you really are, a spiritual spark of Divinity here on earth to create. As you work through these Principles you learn how to direct your Divine expression to consciously create the miracle you want.

If your Heart's Desire is true, then you will focus on it clearly (Principle One). If you focus on it clearly, then you will gain the support of your subconscious mind (Principle Two). If your subconscious mind supports your desire, then you will begin to imagine your desire in great detail (Principle Three). When your imagination creates a blueprint of desire, your conscious mind clears the way to embrace it (Principle Four). When you clear the path of obstructions, you begin to receive inner guidance (Principle

Five). With intuition as your guide, you make enthusiastic and supportive choices (Principle Six). When you choose right actions, faith in the outcome naturally takes over (Principle Seven). And with faith controlling the process, you begin to build your dream with words (Principle Eight).

This then leads you to the last Principle of Creativity. As you approach this final step you are asked to synthesize your efforts and intentions and stay with your dream until it materializes in the physical experience. This is where the final assembly of your dream takes place.

In other words, Principle Number Nine is the process of checking your work on Principles One through Eight to see if you've gathered all the necessary pieces. It tests all your previous efforts, and though no one like to be tested, it is the very activity that guarantees the outcome you want.

The testing phase of creative manifestation is very similar to what happens when you input information into your personal computer. The Universe is very literal in responding to your commands and, like the computer, recognizes that you may change your mind or want to make a correction. Therefore you are given an opportunity before your dream is acted upon to pause, reflect, and evaluate whether or not you really want exactly what you've asked for.

Assembling a dream is no different from assembling anything else—even though you may have all the pieces, until you put them together you do not have what you want. A successful outcome depends on having collected the right pieces at each step along the way. Though the last step may be nothing more than the final turn of a screw, unless everything else before it fits together properly, the screw won't turn. That is the test.

The key is in remaining encouraged, even if you must go back and repeat some earlier steps. It may take several tries. Know that the outcome is waiting to emerge when the pieces come together.

* * *

Many years ago my husband, Patrick, and I, newly married, bought a set of do-it-yourself bookshelves for our first apartment. What was so appealing about this particular set of bookshelves was that the instruction booklet said "Easy Assembly." We took the bookshelves home with all the focus, belief, imagination, commitment, and inspiration necessary to snap those bookshelves together in no time. We enthusiastically opened the box and set to work on the first bookcase. Patrick began to read the instructions, all the while looking at a picture of the finished product.

They began, "Step 1: Begin with Panel A." No problem. I held up Panel A.

"Next, place Panel A and Panel B face-to-face." Easy.

"Insert Bookshelf Panel C into groves at back side between Panel A and Panel B." Trickier, but still following.

"Now slide Panel D underneath the Panel ABC configuration while holding Panel ABC tightly together." What?

We began jockeying Panels A, B, C, and D without success. First C popped out of the groove. Then Panel D dropped from the bottom. Then C fell in again. Finally we managed to get them in order. Our arms entwined, Patrick tried to read the instructions two feet away.

"Snap Panel E into the top of the Panel ABCD configuration."

After reaching for Panel E with his toes and sliding it across the room, all the while yelling at me not to move or breathe, Patrick finally succeeded in maneuvering it into place. It was a little wobbly but starting to look a bit like a bookshelf. We continued.

"Slide Shelf H into middle of ABCDE configuration." Slowly Shelf H slid in, and we thought we were home free. I was holding the bookshelf together as Patrick started manipulating the doors. They wouldn't fit.

"Stop wobbling so hard! It's going to break!" I cried. My arms ached from holding everything together. The doors didn't fit, and as Patrick maneuvered, Panel A popped out. I managed to keep H from falling while Patrick jumped up and grabbed Panel A, only to have Panel E pop out. Suddenly the entire thing collapsed into itself in the middle of the floor! We couldn't believe it. This was much more effort than we had bargained for.

Patrick yelled at me. I yelled at him. He said the thing was defective. I said he couldn't follow instructions. We both sighed, looking at the jumble on the floor, and started all over again, this time with *me* reading the instructions.

I felt smug as I clicked through the instructions, and we progressed. I reached the part where we had to slide the shelf in, and with the tiniest little shove, the whole thing suddenly collapsed again!

Cursing, we started all over again. This went on for what seemed like hours. I called Patrick stupid. He called me stupid. At one point we were convinced that we had the wrong instructions. Then we decided it was a defective bookshelf, and finally we concluded that whoever had written those instructions was a sadistic sicko cackling at us from somewhere back at corporate headquarters. We thought we'd been had—whatever these pieces made, it wasn't a bookshelf!

"What is the problem?" we asked each other, frustrated beyond belief. Several times we were so close and yet so far away. We had been ready to give up many times, except that the picture on the box kept staring at us as if to say "Don't give up. Believe. See it. Feel it. Focus on it. Keep trying!"

I thought for a moment. What could we possibly do better? Then it came to me. "I know. Let's pretend we *are* the bookshelf," I said. "If we were the bookshelf, what would we need to stay together?"

Slowly, methodically, step by step, we went over the instructions. A to B—check. Bottom, C—check. Top, D—check.

As I read D very closely, for the first time I noticed a tiny "*" that looked like a speck of dirt. I looked down at the bottom of the page, where a matching "*" signaled an explanation in the tiniest print possible: "Insert plastic safety locks in holes." In a small package next to the door handles were two plastic safety locks that looked like white beans. I pushed them into two holes.

Voilà! The wobbly assembly instantly became the Rock of Gibraltar. On went the shelf, the doors, the handles, and there it stood like Proud Mary. The shambles on the floor had become a beautiful bookshelf. The second shelf snapped together like magic in less than thirty minutes.

We couldn't help but muse over how the whole thing came together the minutes we became totally focused on the outcome. But in order to reach the final outcome we had to go back to the beginning several times. Knowing that somewhere, somehow, our dream was hidden in that mess on the floor, we never gave up. In spite of all our tests and trials, and many failed attempts and discouraged moments, we backed off, but we didn't quit.

This is the way it works with any Heart's Desires. Only the first miracle is a challenge. Stick with it. Refuse to throw in the towel. Tough out the various bumps in the road and stay on course until the end. *That* is the key to your success.

Principle Number Nine says, Go back to the beginning. Check your work, and be flexible enough to see where you need to make corrections and improvement. Principle Number Nine is quality control and the final step to having your dream.

My mom used to tell us all the time, "Only the first miracle is difficult. The rest are easy."

Principle Number Nine asks that you become completely one with your dream, in spite of tests (and there will be plenty), in spite of appearances (and they are discouraging), turning a deaf ear to input (which you can bet will be negative), and refusing to be stopped (although backing off for renewed perspective is allowed).

BE A DARING INDIVIDUAL

Principle Number Nine means breaking away from general consensus, popular opinion, conventional wisdom, sideline know-it-alls, and psychic saboteurs who are too chicken to try creating their own dreams and so are going to distract themselves by trying to derail yours.

Face it—people like to rain on the creative parade! Take a look at history. No one ever encouraged Leonardo da Vinci. Or the Wright brothers. On Benjamin Franklin, Thomas Edison, Madame Curie... All were dismissed by the experts of their day as fools, dreamers, nuts, and quacks. The average naysayer hasn't changed much over the centuries. There are people even today who still argue that there is not such thing as a soul.

Pity them.

Pray for them.

Avoid them.

But for Pete's sake, don't *consult* them when it comes to your dream! And ignore them when they offer unsolicited advice.

I understand how hard it is not to seek support. Usually you are tempted to seek input when you are most discouraged and need some outside encouragement. It's okay to ask for support. Just be sure to seek supportive sources. Consult only people who believe in you, who want you to succeed, and who have the imagination and ability to cheer you on. If you don't know people like this, then go to the highest source you can find—the support of God. What you need to do at this time is pray and ask for staying power.

Principle Number Nine warns you about the tests and advises you to be prepared for them. I tell my clients to consider these tests part of the sport of life. Facing tests and passing is how we measure our progress. Passing these tests can become part of the fun if you accept them as opportunities for growth. When Patrick and I mused over our success in building the bookshelf, it was the eighteen failures that made success so sweet and the second one so easy.

If you want to create your Heart's Desire, you cannot be a wimp. You cannot be easily intimidated. You cannot give up. Creating your Heart's Desire takes persistence, and it takes courage to break away from the pack and follow your heart.

One of my favorite clients, Billie, came to a Heart's Desire workshop when she was seventy-two years old. Billie had been married for over fifty years to a man she didn't really love but she felt she must stick with anyway. She said her husband was a good man but seemed more like an assignment than a partner. She had seen him through eight years of joblessness, eighteen years of alcoholism, seven years of depression, six years of disability from a bad heart, and fifty years of fear, negativity, and low self-esteem.

While he languished in his own spiritual ignorance, she devoted her entire life to reading metaphysical and spiritual literature, self-help books on alcoholism and codependency, and guides to creative visualization and prosperity as a way to teach him to have a better life.

In spite of her efforts, Billie's husband never improved his outlook. However, she became a well-informed and spiritually dynamic person. She had long ago decided to accept her husband's limitations and use her marriage as an opportunity to practice unconditional love. But in spite of the passing time, Billie secretly held on to a special Heart's Desire to experience passionate love with a true soul mate before her life was over.

When Billie's husband turned eighty-one he suddenly died of a stroke. Billie was shocked, but she admitted she also felt liberated. After fifty-two years of him, she was now able to focus on herself. When she came to the Heart's Desire workshop her goals were to organize her finances, sell her home, and move to Sedona, Arizona. "And," she added, "maybe get a boyfriend!" What I admired most about Billie was that being seventy-two years old didn't stop her from being true to her dream.

Her children had a fit and wondered if she had gone senile, but she had fifty years of fighting experience, so they were no match for her. In less than three months Billie did sell her house, bought a trailer in a trailer park in Sedona, and got a part-time job working at a metaphysical bookstore in the town. Billie recently wrote me the most endearing letter.

She said that one day while she was at work, a handsome older gentleman came into the store and began looking around. He was a rugged-looking man who gave off an aura of clarity and physical well-being. She was attracted to him instantly, although her reaction made her feel silly. She hadn't felt this way about someone in over fifty-three years.

Much to her surprise, the man flirted outrageously with her as he asked about various crystals and books in the shop. After an hour he finally selected a rose quartz crystal heart for purchase, which she rang up at the register. Then, to her embarrassment, he handed it to her and said, "This is for you, lovely lady." And he asked her out for coffee.

She said the minute she touched his hand her whole body lit up like a Christmas tree, buzzing with energy and, yes, passion. Their first date never ended. They took up with each other like long-lost lovers, and in August of 1995 they married in a simple ceremony in Sedona Canyon.

Billie had finally found her Heart's Desire. It waited for her because she didn't give up on it and stuck to her guns.

You won't succeed if you give up your dream before its time. You won't succeed if you ask other people what they think. And you especially won't succeed if you look for the approval or permission of others.

You negotiate away your joy, your inner peace, and your

authentic self when you ride on the wings of general consensus. After all, there really is no free lunch. You give up all chance to be genuinely happy when you decide to be "safe" in the world of popular opinion. I call it to the Land of They. Here are some of Their opinions:

"They say there are more men than women, so true love after thirty-five is .01 percent likely."

"They say there is no cure for lung cancer."

"They say the economy is in a recession and money and jobs are scarce."

"They say artists starve, actors wait tables, and writers can't survive."

The Land of They is a bleak place to live; yet, surprisingly, most of the human race chooses to live there. No one knows who runs the Land of They. There are many foot soldiers who defend Them to the death, but I have yet to meet a general.

There isn't one. *They* don't have the guts to lead. That's why They live there.

Principle Number Nine asks that you leave the Land of They. It asks that you take the Never-Say-Die shuttle to the Land of I-Can-and-I-Will, with the help of God. Principle Number Nine summons you to find the courage to stand apart from the crowd and follow your Heart's Desire, all by yourself.

If you follow Principle Number Nine, you will succeed in creating your miracle. That is certain.

If you don't follow Principle Number Nine, your dream will remain forever just a fantasy. That, too, is certain.

Principle Number Nine asks you to trust that your soul is in charge of your life. It means giving up every last attachment to the familiar patterns of failure. This includes everything you may have hiding in the crevices and corners of your mind, in the shadowy closets of your past, and in the dusty trunks of your emotions.

Turn yourself inside out. Live with absolute certainty that you have the power to create anything that you desire—anything!—because the power you need is the power of the Universe flowing through you.

GIVE AND IT WILL BE GIVEN TO YOU

Principle Number Nine asks you to stop holding yourself back from joy and success and to operate from a sense of complete abundance. The simplest way to do this is to practice the spiritual law "Give and it shall be given to you."

Principle Nine is the Principle of generosity. Starting with you, toward you, and then flowing out toward others, generosity and the ability to give freely reflect your complete understanding of all the Principles of Creativity. When you give freely you consciously affirm the laws of cause and effect. You attract to your life the energy you extend, and the law states, "It will return a thousandfold."

Be generous above all in your kindness and your ability to be loving, for as you do, your capacity to receive will expand. The Universe is limitless, but your ability to partake of its limitless blessings is determined by you. We are like cups that draw from the well of Divine grace. As my mother puts it, "Some of us are big cups, some of us are little cups, and some of us are thimbles!"

Don't be a thimble when you can be a big cup. Expand your capacity to be happy and fulfilled, to create and enjoy your creations, by expanding your heart and generous spirit. Lighten up. Hang loose. Take it easy. Don't sweat the small stuff. Know that you are a holy vessel, a child of the Universe, and all your desires are only a natural urge to exercise our Divinity.

The Universe delivers according to what you order. It can just as easily create big as it can create small. It can just as lovingly create strife as it can create harmony. Remember, your thoughts are not just abstractions. They are actual realities that design the very fabric, texture, and dimension of your experience. Let your thoughts be those of a Divine awareness, rightfully expecting and easily sharing all the gifts the Universe readily offers to you.

WHAT YOU REALLY WANT MAY SURPRISE YOU

Sometimes, no matter what we do, it seems as though we aren't progressing. There are times when no matter how hard we try to realize our dream, we run into stumbling blocks. Whether it is receiving the love you want, the job you desire, the physical state of fitness, or the perfect dwelling, something hidden from your awareness is influencing the process.

If this is the case, consider that perhaps what you desire intellectually may not be what's in your heart. Perhaps you've lost touch with your deepest needs and are misdirected. Don't worry. The loving Universe does know your needs and will lead you back to your right path. Put your ideas on hold for now and have the patience to wait for the gifts the Universe has in store for you.

Let me share a story of someone being thwarted in her efforts, only to discover that a Higher power had a plan and was working on her deepest needs and desires all along.

A client of mine, Amy, had been a newspaper editor for over a decade at a liberal Denver periodical when she finally reached a point of boredom and restlessness. She strongly wanted a change. After much consideration Amy quit her job and began an aggressive job search for a more interesting position.

She applied for a job as a writer for a major newspaper and was well received. She underwent several lengthy interviews with the department head and was feeling quite encouraged about getting the job. On her third interview she was asked to write a piece, which she undertook with great enthusiasm. She submitted the article and then waited confidently for her acceptance.

Two weeks passed and she had not heard back from the boss. Worried, she hesitantly called. The minute the boss said, "Hello,

Amy," her heart fell. His tone gave away his decisions. She was not going to get this job after all. The reason, she was told, was that she was overqualified. A week later she heard that a male in the company had received the position.

Disappointed, she continued her job search. Weeks had passed when she was informed of another very exciting job working on grant proposals, for a well-known not-for-profit organization. She applied immediately and once again was very well received. Two interviews later she let herself get excited again. She was called back for a fourth interview... and then, a week later, she received a letter explaining that the post had gone to someone else.

This time she took the rejection hard. Her Heart's Desire to find a more meaningful job seemed doomed to failure. As a result of these rejections, she was suffering serious self-doubt and a wounded ego, and she became very depressed.

A month later yet another bomb hit. Amy was diagnosed with breast cancer.

In the space of six months her aggressive professional world of power and success had crumbled. Because she wasn't working she had lost her self-esteem and confidence and now was facing the possible loss of her life.

The cancer was a wake-up call for Amy. Suddenly she realized that what she was pursuing with all her energy wasn't really her Heart's Desire at all. Her priorities shifted with lightning speed. Her greatest desire was suddenly what she really had been fighting against all along–time to be herself. She wanted time to relax, time to be with her children, who were still very young. She wanted time to think, and to walk, and simply to be alive. After quitting her job, she had attained her Heart's Desire but hadn't even realized it. And now she was threatened with losing everything.

Amy was lucky. The cancer was caught in time, and six months after a radical mastectomy of both breasts, Amy was given a clean bill of health. She was also given the most wonderful gift anyone could ever ask for—clarity abut what was *really* important to her.

Amy left the newspaper world and moved on to what she always truly desired deep down but never noticed before. She is studying calligraphy, mothering her children, and being available to nurture herself. And, finally, she is happy.

Amy's is a case where the loving goodness of the Universe transcended personal vision and led her to a place where her soul found fulfillment. Amy got much more than she actually asked for and is now living a life that reflects her true Heart's Desire.

If, after doing all you can to achieve your Heart's Desire, you are still struggling, then trust that the Universe is working on your behalf. Turn the entire process over to God. The reality is that you are never really very far from your Heart's Desire if only you will step aside and allow your soul to deliver it back to you. The problem is that perhaps you are unconsciously out of touch with what your soul really desires, and a course correction is taking place.

Even though we are driven to create by our emotional natures, we are fundamentally spiritual beings, and our most important desires nurture our souls. Even though we may not realize it, we come into physical expression with certain spiritual ambitions. We have lessons we want to learn, service we want to make. By fulfilling these original spiritual commitments, we find the kind of security and contentment we are looking for.

Often a crisis can stimulate your sacred memories of what you really desire in your life passage. Sometimes it takes running into a dead end to reorient your thinking and reconnect you with your innermost authentic and heartfelt needs. If you are not progressing, put your efforts into the hands of God and pray.

Show me the way to my Heart's Desire.

Hard as it may be to believe, you will soon discover that a far more profoundly rewarding result awaits you. Though the joy of creating is our spiritual play, the joy of remembering who we really are is the true foundation of our Heart's Desire.

Success stories for Principle Number Nine are everywhere. They are the people who you admire, who have achieved what they desire. They are the people who make you feel happy, who dare to do what they want to do, who believe in themselves and stay focused no matter what. They are the people who are easy and kind and, above all, generous with who they are.

The best story about Principle Number Nine is waiting to be written. It is the success story that will interest you more than any other because it is your *own*. As you apply these Principles one at a time, you can be assured that you will arrive where you dream to be—absolutely. Your Heart's Desire is the Divine making itself known in you. Your longing to create is your soul's expression singing out.

The greatest miracle in creating your Heart's Desire is that you will discover your own magnificence. Like a lantern, you will shine out in your dark world. Your creation will be your reward. The realization of your true self will be your gift to the world.

And so, dear child of the Universe, go into the world prepared to play. You are a Divine child of God—the Universe will go with you. You have guides and keepers, angels and teachers, to help you. You have a cosmic crew to see this through. Laugh, play, and create!

Become completely one with your dream and stay with it until its *birth* day. In daring to live your dream, you become a messenger of the gods. You light the way for others and help turn the wheel of evolution. May all your dreams come true.

This or better—so be it!

PRACTICING THE NINTH PRINCIPLE

KEEP AT IT

Spend at least one hour a week working on your dream, *alone.* This might be some activity that you committed to when working on one of the other Principles but haven't yet completed. It may be an art project that expresses your dream. It may be reading an inspirational or useful book to provide you with guidance or information.

TAKE A BREAK

Take time out if you are banging your head against a wall. Go for a walk, bike ride, run, Rollerblade, mountain hike, or other physical excursion *alone* for twenty minutes to an hour, at least once a week. While on your excursions, contemplate new ways to go about your creative work.

A BIG CUP

As a symbolic reminder to yourself that the Universe will fill the cup of your imagination (no matter what the size), get yourself a very *big cup* for the Universe to fill.

STAY OPEN

Be open to the Universe surprising you with even better results than you asked for. Always ask God for "this or better."

PASS IT ON

As a demonstration of your confidence in the Universal Principles of Creativity, lend a hand, share a smile, donate to your favorite charity, give away what you no longer need. Make space for new abundance to flow into your life.

HAPPILY EVERY AFTER

Write down the fairy tale of your Heart's Desire and give yourself a happy ending. So be it!

....

....

MEDITATION

Find a comfortable spot where you will not be disturbed for a minimum of twenty minutes.

Close your eyes and allow yourself to breathe in deeply and slowly. Notice how wonderful it feels to simply let go and allow your body to relax. As you breathe in, imagine being filled with a golden white light of Divine love. As you exhale, allow yourself to remember who you really are—a Divine being, made in the image and likeness of god.

Bringing this full power of creative expression to your conscious mind, affirm the following truths about yourself.

- I am a spiritual channel for creative expression.
- My subconscious mind supports fully my deepest desires and dreams.
- My imagination is limitless, supplying all the ways to embody my dreams.
- I willingly let go of all contrary attachments, obstacles, and thoughts.
- I am fully receptive to my higher wisdom and spiritual guidance.
- I choose with clarity and intelligence ways to bring about my dream.
- I surrender my personal will to channel Divine will through my awareness.

- I speak with integrity, intention, and power as I build my dream in the physical plane.
- I synthesize all my efforts into a graceful creative process.
- I rightfully receive all that I can possibly imagine. *So be it!*

A FINAL SUGGESTION

People have different temperaments and styles when working on their dreams. Some like to work privately, while others have a hard time alone and need the support and community of a group. If you work best alone, enjoy your process. If you prefer to work with others, ask a few friends (everyone is fine) to create your own Heart's Desire group. Alone or with others, the Principles bring results! Above all, have fun *creating the life you really want!*

CREATING THE LIFE YOU REALLY WANT WITH OTHERS

PREPARE Agree to gather for nine sessions of approximately two hours. You will spend one session on each principle. Read the chapter for each principle before you come to the meeting.

DISCUSS Use the time together to discuss what the principle means to you and to hear what it means to others.

REPORT Report how you have applied the principle you have been working on since your last meeting.

ASK FOR SUPPORT Ask for suggestions for those principles with which you have trouble. Working in the group allows you to recognize which principles you are able to execute easily, as to uncover your blind spots.

WORK WITH LOVE Be generous and gentle with yourself and your dreams and those of others. Use this sacred space to create without censorship.

STICK WITH IT Stay true to your group until you have completed all nine principles, even when it seems impossible.

FOLLOW UP WITH PARTY PLANS Agree to a follow-up session (perhaps one year later) to celebrate your successes!

For further information regarding Sonia's workshop, please contact:

Sonia Choquette • Inner Wisdom • 5756 North Ridge Avenue •
Suite 8 • Chicago, IL 60660 • 773-989-1151
www.SoniaChoquette.com

Many Blessings,
Sonia

ABOUT THE AUTHOR

Sonia Choquette is a world-renowned intuitive and spiritual teacher who specializes in helping others recognize that we are all endowed with a sixth sense that we can count on. A masterful teacher committed to strengthening intuition in our daily lives, she is the bestselling author of ten books, including *Ask Your Guides*, *Trust Your Vibes*, *The Answer is Simple...*, *Travelling at the Speed of Love* and *The Psychic Pathway*.

A highly trained intuitive, with extensive background in the mysticism of East and West, Sonia was educated at the University of Denver and at the Sorbonne in Paris, and holds a PhD in metaphysics. Sonia's mission is to help people integrate a strong and trustworthy intuition into their daily lives. She guides them in how to build a psychic scaffolding to support their sixth sense so they can be bigger than they've ever thought possible. She teaches that our psychic sense's primary function is to guide our soul's growth and keep us connected to our path and purpose. Without its direction we lose our way. In her first book, *The Psychic Pathway*, Sonia states, "The psychic pathway is the pathway of the soul. It is a pathway of life lived with the belief and understanding that you are a soul, and that spiritual growth is your primary purpose."

Sonia's own path has encompassed numerous bestselling books published in more than 23 countries, speaking and conducting workshops around the globe, thousands of grateful clients and a home in Chicago that she shares with husband Patrick Tully, daughters Sonia and Sabrina, and a poodle named Miss T.

www.soniachoquette.com

HAY HOUSE TITLES OF RELATED INTEREST

DAVID WELLS' COMPLETE GUIDE TO DEVELOPING YOUR PSYCHIC SKILLS, by David Wells

DEVELOPING MEDIUMSHIP, by Gordon Smith

THE DREAM WHISPERER: *Unlock the Power of Your Dreams*, by Davina MacKail

THE INTELLIGENT GUIDE TO THE 6TH SENSE, by Heidi Sawyer

THE MAP: Finding the Magic and Meaning in Your Life, by Colette Baron-Reid

YOU KNOW MORE THAN YOU THINK: How to Access Your Super-Subconscious Powers, by Seka Nikolic

All of the above are available at your local bookshop, or may be ordered by contacting Hay House (see overleaf).